W9-BHY-188

Warren Bennis

A WARREN BENNIS BOOK

This collection of books is devoted exclusively to new and exemplary contributions to management thought and practice. The books in this series are addressed to thoughtful leaders, executives, and managers of all organizations who are struggling with and committed to responsible change. My hope and goal is to spark new intellectual capital by sharing ideas positioned at an angle to conventional thought—in short, to publish books that disturb the present in the service of a better future.

Nathaniel Branden
Foreword by Warren Bennis

• •

Self-Esteem at Work

How Confident People Make Powerful Companies

Jossey-Bass Publishers
San Francisco

Jossey-Bass books and products are available through most bookstores. To contact Jossey-Bass directly, call (888) 378–2537, fax to (800) 605–2665, or visit our website at www.josseybass.com.

Substantial discounts on bulk quantities of Jossey-Bass books are available to corporations, professional associations, and other organizations. For details and discount information, contact the special sales department at Jossey-Bass.

For sales outside the United States, please contact your local Simon & Schuster International Office.

TCF Manufactured in the United States of America on Lyons Falls Turin Book. This paper is acid-free and 100 percent totally chlorine-free.

Library of Congress Cataloging-in-Publication Data

Branden, Nathaniel.
Self-esteem at work: how confident people make powerful companies / Nathaniel Branden, Warren Bennis. — 1st ed.
p. cm.
ISBN 0-7879-4001-1 (acid-free paper)
1. Career development. 2. Self-esteem. 3. Leadership. I. Bennis, Warren G. II. Title.
HF5381 .B639 1998
658.4'09—ddc21 98-9087

FIRST EDITION
HB Printing 10 9 8 7 6 5 4 3 2 1

Contents

Foreword

I am absurdly delighted to inaugurate this new Jossey-Bass series with Nathaniel Branden's latest book, *Self-Esteem at Work*. Full disclosure, I suppose, dictates that I should tell you that I have known of Nathaniel's work for many years and was a fan long before meeting him. Shortly after I moved to Los Angeles almost twenty years ago, we became best friends, spending long hours discussing and arguing about life, about organizations, about politics, about leadership, and about—well, you knew it was coming—self-esteem. I found him a kindred spirit and a rich, complex mind, always alive with ideas and with an awesome capacity to test every assumption and joust with conventional wisdom. I'll never forget my first long conversation with him; it was like opening up your first bottle of champagne. I like the way his mind works.

For years, I have been urging him to apply his ideas to the workplace. Other activities got in the way and made that impossible. Finally, he acquiesced. Obviously, I'm pleased, pleased because I know of few issues, perhaps no other issue, that so clearly and unfailingly influences the success or failure of our organizations in our New Economy—this spastic, turbulent, confusing, unsettling, messy, awesomely complex world we are creating and participating in—than self-esteem.

The premise of Branden's book is that intellectual capital—the home page of ideas and imagination—will be the single most important factor in achieving competitive advantage in the next millennium. And because of the primacy of intellectual capital, the need for self-esteem has acquired a new economic urgency—and this fact has profound implications for leadership and management. Further, that the key to unleashing and deploying that engine will be the capacity of leaders and their institutions to generate self-esteem in the workplace. And, finally, that knowledge workers, in particular, can be creative and productive and happy only in an environment that nurtures self-esteem. This book goes a long way to teach us about how self-esteem can be brought into existence and sustained. Quite an achievement.

Branden writes with unfailing lucidity. I've never known anyone who writes the way he speaks, in complete—nay, not just sentences—but complete paragraphs. He also builds surely on his previous accomplishments in psychology, philosophy, and economics. Something else comes to mind. There is a resonant Emersonian beat to his lyric, a celebration of that insouciant American self, that invincible entrepreneurial spirit that throbs throughout these pages.

This new series of books, to which I proudly give my name, is based on the premise that ideas ultimately govern behavior. I am certain that self-esteem, if taken seriously and implemented, will enhance not only our working lives but the magnanimity embedded in the human spirit.

Santa Monica, California Warren Bennis
May 1998

Preface

The theme of this book is the new importance of self-esteem in an information economy, and the practical implications of that importance for leaders, managers, and anyone seeking conscious control over his or her career.

By self-esteem I mean the experience of being competent to cope with the basic challenges of life and of being worthy of happiness. This means trust in your ability to think, learn, make appropriate decisions, and respond effectively to new conditions. It also means confidence in your right to experience success and personal fulfillment—the conviction that happiness is appropriate for you.

Self-esteem pertains to an experience of efficacy. This entails confidence in your mind at a very deep level. Not the confidence of knowing you can perform this or that task appropriately. Not confidence in how much you may know about any particular subject. Rather, it means trust in the processes by which you reason, understand, learn, choose, decide, and regulate action.

It is a trust that cannot be faked. It has to be reality-based—has to be earned. How it is earned is one of the issues I will examine.

Self-esteem has always been an important psychological need, ever since we evolved the capacity for abstract self-awareness. Now, however, in a way that was not true in the past, it has become an urgent economic need.

I will consider the nature and dynamics of self-esteem and its role in behavior and motivation, both personal and professional, in Chapter Two. We cannot understand how and why self-esteem has acquired its new importance in the workplace if we do not understand what self-esteem is and how it operates. But first, in Chapter One, I examine how the workplace has changed—the new and unprecedented challenges that individuals and business organizations face, and how these challenges relate to self-esteem.

Self-esteem has become an urgent economic need.

Following these two chapters, I will consider the implications of the new realities for leadership, management practice, and the requirements of creating a high-performance organization characterized by continuous innovation and sustained profitability—in a ferociously competitive global marketplace.

Finally, I will examine the intimate linkage between working on your own development as a human being and striving to make yourself and your organization adaptive to the challenges of an economy that seems more ruthlessly demanding with every passing year. The message here is that work itself can be approached as a path to personal growth, so that self-esteem and professional competence can rise together and reinforce each other—while one avoids the error of identifying personal worth with career success.

The net result is a guidebook for working with self and others in a business environment.

• • • • • • •

Business has often been skeptical of the intrusion of psychology into its domain. Understandably so. A great deal of what has been offered to the business community as "psychology" has had very little to recommend it. And some of the early attempts to introduce "personal growth work" into business—remember, for example, the early T-groups or encounter groups—led in some cases to employees feeling emotionally invaded and even damaged; it also led, in a few instances, to lawsuits. So if business is skeptical about the offerings of psychologists, it is wise to be—or, if not skeptical, then at least cautious and thoughtful. And yet, business cannot avoid psychology because it cannot avoid the question of what must be done to motivate people to give their best.

Executives do not ask, "How can we establish an organizational culture that nurtures self-esteem?" They do ask, "How can we establish an organizational culture that supports high performance, personal accountability, and creative initiative?" The questions are different, yet the answers are essentially the same.

Although I have written a great deal about self-esteem in the past, this book assumes no familiarity with my earlier writings and is entirely self-contained. When necessary, I have permitted myself to borrow material from my previous books because I am aware I may be addressing executives who have never read anything in the field of psychology in general or self-esteem in particular.

◆ ◆ ◆ ◆ ◆ ◆ ◆

I owe the genesis of this book, in part, to an encounter I had about fifteen years ago, before I began doing corporate consulting. I was conducting a self-esteem seminar for the general public at which six or seven business consultants were participants. It turned out they all knew one another and they invited me to lunch. I expressed interest in what had inspired them to take this particular course. Here is the essence of what they said:

"We feel something is missing in our consulting practice. We can design a program for an organization, elicit people's initial enthusiasm, and pretty soon they are seeing with their own eyes that the program works and produces desired results—and yet, after a while, they stop doing it and revert to their old ways. It's as if their self-concept—the way they view themselves and what's appropriate to them—can't accommodate this new way of being and doing. Somehow, it's not who they think they are. Their attitude seems to be, 'I'm just not a person who does things this way.' That's an issue of self-esteem, isn't it? So that's why we're here—to learn more about the principles of self-esteem and perhaps to learn if there's any way to incorporate self-esteem ideas in our work."

These consultants had grasped a profoundly important principle—that it is very difficult for people to act beyond their deepest vision of who and what they believe themselves to be. They may succeed in doing so for brief periods of time, but if their self-concept remains unchanged, the gravitational pull of their self-limiting beliefs will draw them back to old, familiar, and less productive ways of functioning. It was from that encounter on that I began thinking more and more about the application of my work in self-esteem to the world of business.

It is very difficult for people to act beyond who and what they believe themselves to be.

The problem raised by these consultants, important though it is, reflects only one of the ways that issues of self-esteem show up in the workplace. There are many others.

A simple example is the fact that analyses of business failure tell us that a common cause is executives' fear of making decisions. What is fear of making decisions but lack of confidence in one's mind and judgment? In other words, a problem of self-esteem.

Yet another example pertains to competence at negotiating. A study discloses that whereas people with healthy self-esteem tend to be realistic in their demands, negotiators with poor self-esteem tend to ask for too much or too little (depending on other personality variables)—but in either case being less effective than they could be.

More broadly, interpersonal competence—so important in corporate settings today—tends to be adversely affected by low self-esteem. Persons suffering from deep insecurities and self-doubts tend to behave in inappropriate and counterproductive ways in their dealings with others, whether this means being overcontrolling and gratuitously combative or timid and oversolicitous. Instead of being task-focused, too often they focus on self-aggrandizement or self-protection; either way, their relations with others are adversarial rather than benevolent. Far more than lack of technical knowledge or ability, this problem is a major cause of career breakdown.

There is virtually no aspect of business activity—from leading to managing to participating in teams, and from dealing with customers to engaging in research and development to responding to new challenges and new ideas—that is not significantly affected by the level of one's self-esteem.

What is fear of making decisions but lack of confidence in one's mind and judgment?

For this reason, everyone involved in the process of production, from CEO to first-time employee, can benefit from an understanding of the principles and strategies that follow.

Los Angeles, California Nathaniel Branden
May 1998

Acknowledgments

My thanks, first and foremost, to my friend and colleague Warren Bennis, who persuaded me to write this book. From the time that he learned of my interest in applying self-esteem principles and technology to the problems and challenges of the modern business organization, Warren has been my guide, mentor, and cheerleader. I am appreciative also of his right-on-target editorial suggestions.

Next, I want to thank my editor, Cedric Crocker, for his wisdom as an editor and also for his benevolent patience when other responsibilities prevented me from the completing this book as quickly as we both would have liked.

Thanks to my agent, Nat Sobel, for his feedback on the book, his helpful suggestions, and, more broadly, for the consistency of his support of my career.

Finally, my gratitude to my wife, Devers, first for always offering stimulating feedback on my writing, and second, for her good-humored acceptance at dinner parties (and elsewhere) when she sees my eyes glazing over and knows that I am at work on a book.

Self-Esteem at Work

1

The Twenty-First Century Workplace

An individual who experiences profound doubts about his or her ability to think, understand, learn, or cope with the basic challenges of life is at a severe disadvantage—at any time or place in history—especially when confronted with the new and unfamiliar. An individual who experiences profound doubts about his or value as a human being, who feels unworthy or undeserving of friendship, respect, love, achievement, success, fulfillment—in a word, happiness—is, again, at a severe disadvantage, especially when it comes to asserting legitimate needs and protecting legitimate interests.

And yet, the need for self-esteem acquires new urgency in an information economy. Why?

To understand the answer, we must understand some of the most important ways in which the world has changed.

The Information Age

In the past several decades, extraordinary developments have occurred in the American and global economies. The United States has shifted from a manufacturing society to an information society. Mind work has replaced physical labor as the dominant employee activity. We now live in a global economy characterized by rapid change, accelerating scientific and technological breakthroughs, and an unprecedented level of competitiveness.

Everyone recognizes that these developments create demands for higher levels of education and training than were required of previous generations. What is not generally recognized is that these developments also create new demands on our psychological resources. Specifically, these developments ask us to bring a greater capacity for innovation, self-management, and personal responsibility—a higher level of consciousness—to our work activities.

This is not just asked at the top. It is asked at every level of a business enterprise, from senior management to first-line supervisor and even to entry-level personnel.

Here is a description of the position of manufacturing production operator at Motorola, an entry-level job: "Analyze computer reports and identify problems through experiments and statistical process control. Communicate manufacturing performance metrics to management, and understand the company's competitive position."[1]

Although many organizations fiercely resist accepting it and struggle to hang on to a time that is irretrievably gone, a modern business can no longer be run by a few people who think and many people who do what they are told—the traditional military command-and-control model. Today, organizations require not only a higher level of knowledge and skill among all those who participate in the process of production, but also a higher level of independence, self-reliance, self-trust, and capacity to exercise initiative—in a word, self-esteem. This means that in the process of wealth-creation, persons with a decent level of self-esteem are now needed in large numbers.

To see this fact in perspective and appreciate its full significance, let us review—very briefly—the earlier stages of our economic development.

Twenty Thousand Years Ago

Imagine that you live in a world that does not yet know agriculture—say, twenty thousand years ago, when human beings lived as nomads and survived by gathering, foraging, and hunting. This was the earliest manner of human survival.

Until very recently, intelligence was a luxury unrelated to the raw realities of survival.

In *The Ascent of Man*, Jacob Bronowski describes this form of existence as follows:

> It is not possible in the nomad life to make things that will not be needed for several weeks. They could not be carried. And in fact [nomads] did not know how to make them. . . . There is no room for innovation, because there is not time, on the move, between evening and morning, coming and going all their lives, to develop a new device or a new thought—or even a new tune. The only habits that survive are the old habits. The only ambition of the son is to be like the father.
>
> It is a life without features. Every day is the end of a day like the last, and every morning will be the beginning of a journey like the day before.[2]

It is not a world in which your sense of self is daily challenged by new demands on your efficacy. In fact, in its modern meaning, it is doubtful that you yet have "a sense of self." Concepts such as individuality or personal identity do not yet exist, although the feelings and images that are their precursors almost certainly lie submerged in your psyche. As best we can conjecture, there is nothing in your experience that will relate your ability to survive to your inventiveness or creativity, or that will raise the question, Is my way of functioning appropriate to the requirements of my life and well-being?

Agricultural Civilization

Civilization began only with the change from a nomad existence to village agriculture—between twelve thousand and ten thousand years ago—when groups of human beings settled in small geographical areas and learned to extract their sustenance from the earth. Now began the agonizingly slow process of inventing the early tools. Life was still endless repetition, almost entirely devoid of change within the life span of individuals. Changes occurred not over years but over hundreds of years, even millennia. The cultivation of wheat, the invention of the plow, the domestication of animals, the development of wheel and axle, each a landmark in our cultural history, are achievements separated by many centuries. For the average man or woman living ten thousand years ago, seven thousand years ago, three thousand years ago, or even a few hundred years ago, life and survival were still, as for the early nomads, a matter of mastering a few basic skills passed down for generations—of imitating motions that no one alive had originated.

Of course, even to master those motions required a process of thought. For all living species that possess it, consciousness is the basic tool of survival. However, survival was seen more as a challenge to strength, stamina, speed, and agility—and the grace of the gods—than to intelligence. No such concept as intelligence existed. The relation of mind to adaptiveness had not yet been grasped. The concept of mind itself had not yet been grasped.

It was only a few hundred years before the common era, in Ancient Greece, that reason and mind were for the first time identified explicitly. Prior to that philosophical achievement, there was consciousness but not yet abstract self-consciousness. Men and women thought but they did not think about thinking. They made rational connections but did not grasp the idea of integration. They did not identify mind as their basic tool of survival. The concept of efficacy lay in the distant future—as did the concept of self-esteem and its relationship to the task of meeting life's challenges, including the challenge of survival itself.

Even the great Aristotle, father of logic, who saw farther than anyone had seen before, believed the noblest activity of reason lay in the contemplation of eternal truths—certainly not in improving the quality of life on earth through productive work. He did not conceive the mind as a continuing source of invention, innovation, and progress, and historically could not have done so. The concept of progress did not yet exist.

Not advances in agriculture, or the emergence of cities, or the opening of trade routes, inspired in anyone the idea of progress that we take for granted. Life was perceived as essentially unchanging. If you lived, say, one thousand years ago, you did not expect the future to be better than the past, except, perhaps, in heaven. You did not expect life to become easier or richer in what it had to offer. You had no anticipation that new inventions or discoveries might transform your world.

In A.D. 1000, fully as much as in 1000 B.C., people expected their grandchildren's lives to be the same as their own—and their own generally mirrored that of their ancestors.

Throughout all the millennia past, until very, very recently, work meant physical labor, not mental work. Intelligence, like education, was perceived as a luxury, unrelated to the raw realities of existence and requirements of survival.

In the Judeo-Christian world, the Bible taught that the necessity to work for a living was God's punishment for man's disobedience. Exiled from Eden where his needs were filled effortlessly and automatically, man was condemned to earn his daily bread by the sweat of his brow. The unmistakable implication was that work is a curse. And that was how work was perceived: as a grim requirement that made you old very quickly; certainly not as a source of joy or a means of self-expression or self-fulfillment, or as a path to self-development.

Self-expression, self-fulfillment, and self-development are ideas that have a meaning to the contemporary Western mind almost incomprehensible to men and women in preindustrial times. These ideas remain incomprehensible in parts of the world where grinding poverty and disease are the central and overwhelming reality of human existence and neither industrialism nor capitalism has gained a foothold. Like self-esteem, such ideas are the products of an individualist culture.

In preindustrial cultures—from the world of hunters and gatherers to that of feudal serfs—there was neither a market for the independent mind nor much (if any) economic need for self-esteem. There was no market demand for intelligence, self-responsibility, communication skills, interpersonal competence, innovativeness, creativity, or the entrepreneurial mentality. Indeed, in medieval times, not only did traits such as self-esteem or self-assertiveness ordinarily confer no particular economic benefits—except, perhaps, for a handful of merchants, traders, explorers, and artists—they could be positively life-endangering: they could lead their possessors to the torture rack or the stake.

If you lived a thousand years ago, you were almost certainly born into a distinct and unchangeable place in the social order. With very rare exceptions, you did not choose an occupation but rather were cast by circumstances of birth into the role of peasant, artisan, or knight—or the wife of one. Your sense of identity, such as it was, derived not from your choices and actions, not from your achievements, but from seeing yourself as an integral part of "the natural order," which was presumed to be ordained by God. Subject to the vicissitudes of war, famine, and plague, you were more or less guaranteed a livelihood, determined by tradition. There was very little competition, just as there was very little economic freedom, or any other kind of freedom. Yours was not a world that valued self-assertiveness, understood individuality, admired self-responsibility, grasped political liberty or the "Rights of Man," imagined innovativeness as a way of life, appreciated the relation of mind, intelligence, and creativity to survival, or had a place for self-esteem. The system on which your well-being depended expected little of you but obedience and conformity.

The Birth of Individualism

Our idea of the individual as an autonomous, self-determining entity, able to think independently and bear responsibility for his or her existence, emerged from several historical developments: the Renaissance in the fifteenth century, the Reformation in the sixteenth, and the Enlightenment in the eighteenth—and their two offspring, the Industrial Revolution and capitalism.

Against the long night of the Dark and Middle Ages, the slogan of the Renaissance was "the right to see"—the right to that "lust of the eyes" (the desire for knowledge) denounced by Augustine. In philosophy, the right to study the universe and man's place in it. In science, the right to study physical nature, with the rebirth of such forbidden sciences as anatomy and astronomy. In art, the right to study this earth and to depict the full reality of the human body, of nature, of perspective, of three-dimensionality, as perceived by our senses.

With the Reformation, individuals gained a new measure of independence.

The Reformation broke the monopoly of the Catholic Church through the rise of the Protestant churches—a victory made possible by the invention of the printing press, which gave people direct, personal access to the teachings of their religion. A new measure of independence, however modest, however restricted, was conceded to the individual.

The essence of the Enlightenment was its celebration of reason, science, liberty (although with conflicting notions as to what these terms meant), and the values of secular existence—its esteem for life on earth.

The Industrial Revolution, the introduction of machinery into the process of production, was the expression of human intelligence now placed in the service of improving the conditions of material existence. The capitalist system that emerged with it was characterized by free markets and open competition, in which goods and services were produced for profit, labor was performed for wages, and the means of production and distribution were privately owned. Its corollary was political freedom; historically, its development was linked to the doctrine of individual rights, especially in the United States. In fact, a fully consistent capitalism cannot exist without recognition of these rights, as I discuss in *Taking Responsibility*.[3]

It was from this period forward that evidence began to accumulate illuminating the relationship between survival (or economic adaptiveness) and the creative exercise of mind. And it was from this period forward that the issue of self-esteem began growing in economic significance—although still very far away from what its significance would be by the final decades of the twentieth century.

With the Industrial Revolution, self-esteem began growing in economic significance.

With the birth of capitalism and the increasing emergence of merchants, shopkeepers, tradesmen, and early American entrepreneurs, a number of shifts in people's consciousness took place—shifts in the consciousness of the culture, one might say.

The question, What has your birth determined you to be? was

replaced by the question, What have you made of yourself? Identity was no longer something you inherited but something you created and were accountable for.

Identity was no longer something you inherited but something you created and were accountable for.

The idea of progress ignited people's imagination. The premise was that intelligence, perseverance, ingenuity, and enterprise could generate a continuing improvement in the standard of living—that new discoveries, new products, new expressions of creativity could without limit keep raising the quality of human existence. Mind was not yet fully understood to be the supreme capital asset—far from it—but nonetheless it had begun to move from background to foreground, sometimes under such names as *competence* or *ability*.

Self-reliance and self-responsibility were seen as appropriate to the new order of things, in contrast to the conformity and obedience more valued in earlier tribal societies.

New ideas with commercial application were valued. The ability to perceive and actualize new wealth-producing possibilities was valued. The entrepreneurial mentality was rewarded.

All such developments represented new challenges to people's self-esteem—to their deepest vision of their competence and worth. Born into this new world, you might wonder, Am I equal to the demands and possibilities of life?

To some, this was an exhilarating question; to others, a terrifying one.

The Industrial Age

The large organizations that we associate with modern capitalism emerged in the United States only after the Civil War and in

Europe after the Franco-Prussian War—only in roughly the last 135 years. Throughout the nineteenth century, we remained predominately an agricultural economy; most people earned their living off the land, and land was perceived as the chief source of wealth, as it had been for thousands of years. We began as a nation of farmers and small shopkeepers.

And the average farmer or shopkeeper was not an innovator. He was perhaps more self-reliant than his ancestors, more independent and resourceful—evidenced by the facts, among others, that he may have left his homeland in Europe to make a new life in America, and that the looser social structure in the New World, the greater freedom, threw him more on his own and demanded greater self-direction and therefore greater self-esteem. But within the knowledge context of the period, economic adaptiveness demanded of him neither high levels of education nor of innovativeness. His mind, learning ability, and decision-making capabilities were not constantly challenged. He survived principally by performing simple and basic tasks he had been taught by others. The economic system did not require more of him than that for its effective functioning.

Entrepreneurs and inventors were still an infinitesimally small minority.

The individuals who did see themselves challenged in new ways and were inspired to meet the challenges—the entrepreneurs and inventors—were an infinitesimally small minority. It was they who were responsible for the transition from an agricultural to a manufacturing society. This led to U.S. leadership in steel, electricity, the telephone and telegraph, farm equipment and agronomy, office equipment, the first household appliances, and, a little later, automobiles and aviation.

Compared with the rate of change today, change still proceeded very slowly (although it was proceeding very quickly compared with earlier centuries). To give an example of how much the world has developed in the last hundred years: toward the end of the nineteenth century, the head of the U.S. Patent Office proposed that the office be closed because everything that could be invented had already been invented!

Through all the centuries and millennia of our history, until only a few seconds ago, measured in evolutionary time, the common assumption was that everything that could be known was already known. Contrast that perspective with our perspective today.

If you lived and worked in say, 1905, the likelihood was that you earned your living either as a farmer or as a domestic servant; this was how most people earned their living at that time. If you left the land or domestic service for a factory job, you found that industrial jobs required neither new skills you did not already possess nor any specialized knowledge. Once again, you supported yourself by performing simple physical tasks exactly as you had been taught—with nothing more required, intellectually or psychologically. You worked shorter hours than you had as a farmer or servant, and for better pay. And you worked a specific number of hours known to you in advance, which was never the case in your previous employment. Only with the advent of the factory system were you assured some stretch of time you could safely call your own.

Difficult as the early years of the factory system were, judged by contemporary standards, you were likely to perceive a factory job as an opportunity—a step upward, a chance to lift the quality of life relative to what you had known before. (In denunciations of the early factory system, this fact tends to be forgotten; too often we judge the past by the standards of today rather than in the context of the time.)

What is worth noting, however, is that the requirements for economic adaptiveness had not significantly changed. It might take a farmer or domestic servant a year or two to master the essentials of the work, whereas it took a machine operator only a few weeks. But in either case, that was the end of it: no new learning was demanded. No innovativeness was expected. Obedience and reliability were at a premium, not resourcefulness.

Obedience and reliability were still at a premium, not resourcefulness.

To be sure, if you were an ambitious and imaginative person, with a good level of self-esteem—if you were more conscious, more self-assertive, and more self-responsible than those around you—you would very likely see possibilities for advancement that others did not. You might become the successful owner of your own business or enter a profession such as law or medicine. In a free or even a semi-free society, self-esteem always confers advantages. But you would still be one of a small minority. Your psychology was not yet what the system needed in large numbers.

In the early years of our industrial history, the owner more or less knew everything needed to run his business. He might need the assistance of a few other people to carry out the work, but not because they had mastered knowledge of which he was ignorant. As businesses grew and technology advanced, companies began to employ managers and engineers with particular areas of mastery outside the boss's. But still, knowledge was confined to a very few. Thinking and decision-making were done at the top of the hierarchy and passed down the chain of command.

If you worked in such an organization you were told what was expected of you and your sole responsibility was to carry out instructions. An ideal employee would be one whose actions matched the consistency and reliability of the machines; this was the standard against which you were measured. No one expected you to come up with valuable ideas or suggestions for the operating of the business. Except in the most restricted sense, no one expected you to think.

Looked at from the perspective of today, it is easy enough to criticize what is now called "classical management." Understood in its historical context, we can appreciate its logic and benefits. If you were working on an assembly line in, say, 1912, and if you were unable to read or write English—you were an immigrant from the Old World—by conscientiously carrying out the task you had been trained to do, you could earn a living for yourself and your family. And it was a better and more reliable living than had ever been possible to you before.

Frederick Taylor's great innovation was to analyze production tasks into simple, discrete, easily mastered steps, which no one had thought of doing before, and which allowed you to work "smarter" rather than harder. Raising your productivity, Taylor's methods raised your wages.

Thus blue-collar employees of even modest self-esteem could learn to function effectively in an environment created for them, as it were, by those whose self-confidence, ability, and ambition were higher.

As technology evolved, the demand for more advanced levels of skill in the operation of equipment increased. Yet there was no great demand for higher education or creative thinking or self-management—or autonomy. Such values might make a substantial personal contribution to your life, in terms of enjoyment and satisfaction, but not in terms of your income. Not in the 1950s or 1960s, at the climax of the industrial phase of our development, when the blue-collar worker was at the pinnacle of success. Then, most college-educated men and women did not earn more than a skilled machinist who was a high school dropout, often of quite limited intellectual development.

Of course, many more opportunities existed for an ambitious, high-self-esteeming individual of superior ability. One of the great achievements of capitalism, differentiating it from all earlier forms of organization, was that it created a market for the independent mind. In that sense, self-esteem now did make a difference, economically as well as personally.

But in terms of what business firms were looking for, the 1950s and 1960s were the time of the "Organization Man." Not independent thinking but faithful compliance with the rules was the road to success. Not to stand out but to fit in was the formula for those who wanted to rise. Just enough self-esteem to maintain a decent level of competence within the framework that existed—but not so much self-esteem as to question or challenge basic company values and policies.

The 1950s and 1960s were the time of the "Organization Man."

Business itself—large business—had become heavily bureaucratic, weighted down with many levels of management. It depended more on economies of scale than on innovation to maintain economic supremacy, indulging much undetected waste and moving further and further away from the entrepreneurial spirit of an earlier age. (Government policies played a major role in bringing this development about, but that is another story.) Alfred Sloan, famed head of General Motors, once summed up the carmaker's strategy by saying that "it was not necessary to lead in technical design or run the risk of untried experiments, provided that our cars were at least equal in design to the best of our competitors in the grade."[4] One of the last great innovations of the American automobile industry was the automatic transmission—introduced in 1939.

In the decades following World War II, the United States was the undisputed industrial leader of the world. We were at the height of our economic power. With the other industrial nations struggling to recover from the wreckage of the war, we had no competitors. Our workers were the highest paid. Our standard of living was beyond most of the world's imagination, if not beyond its envy.

Communist and socialist countries were promising someday to surpass us, but that was only a promise for the future with nothing to support it in the present, although it was a promise that many American and European intellectuals believed and propagated and were astonishingly slow to question.

Our economic complacency during the 1950s and 1960s was both understandable and dangerous. Challenges were coming that we did not foresee and for which we were little prepared. Not from the Soviet Union and its satellites, which in future decades would collapse under the weight of their own contradictions and self-destructive policies, but from such interrelated phenomena as the invention of the microchip, the explosion in personal computing and telecommunications, and the emergence of a global economy.

The Mind Millennium

The changes in the national and world economy that represent the greatest challenge to our resourcefulness, and have the greatest significance for our self-esteem, may be summarized as follows:

1. *The shift from a manufacturing to an information economy, the diminishing need for manual or blue-collar workers, and the rapidly growing need for knowledge workers with advanced verbal, mathematical, and social skills.*

Just as we produce far more agricultural products than in the past with far fewer agricultural workers, so we are manufacturing more goods than ever before in our history but with far fewer people. More and more, physical labor is replaced by knowledge work.

Today, in a complex business organization that orchestrates the knowledge and skills of financial, marketing, and sales people with engineers, lawyers, systems analysts, mathematicians, chemists, physicists, researchers, designers, health care professionals, experts of every kind—what we see is no longer management and workers but an integration of specialists. Each of these specialists has knowledge and expertise not possessed by others in the organization, including the boss. Each is relied on to think, to create, to be innovative, to contribute. Workers have become "associates" in an atmosphere that is becoming increasingly more collegial rather than hierarchical.

Whereas independence, creativity, self-responsibility, and interpersonal competence are at a high premium, mechanical obedience per se is worth very little. This is one of the chief reasons that, in the economic sphere, self-esteem is now challenged—and needed—far more than at earlier stages of our development.

2. *The continuing and escalating explosion of new knowledge, new technology, and new products and services, which keeps raising the requirements of economic adaptiveness.*

In the 1990s, successful business organizations know that to remain competitive in world markets they need a steady stream of innovation in products, services, and internal systems that must be planned for as a normal part of their operations. Thoughtful individuals know that if they wish to advance in their careers they cannot rest on yesterday's knowledge and skills. An overattachment to the known and familiar has become costly and dangerous; it threatens both organizations and individuals with obsolescence.

Both organizations and individuals are threatened with obsolescence.

Scientific and technological discoveries are pouring from our laboratories and research and development departments at an unprecedented rate—challenging us to do better and better and to think and respond faster and faster, and challenging our belief in our competence to do so.

3. *The emergence of a global economy of unprecedented competitiveness, which is yet another challenge to our ingenuity and belief in ourselves.*

When, by 1953, Japan completed its postwar reconstruction, it embarked on an extraordinary pattern of growth that averaged 9.7 percent annually over the next twenty years. Leading this explosion was the triumph of the Japanese automobile, but that success was far from an isolated feat. Japan became the leading producer of radios in the 1960s and of television sets in the 1970s. Japanese products became associated with high quality and dependability, most notably in high-technology areas. By the 1980s, the United States was facing competition not only from Japan but other Pacific Rim countries as well: South Korea, Singapore, Taiwan, and Hong Kong. That was from the East. From the opposite direction there was a reborn and regenerated Europe—above all, an industrially powerful and fast-growing West Germany.

American business at first reacted with dismay, disbelief, and denial. Global competitiveness of this intensity was a new and disorienting experience. Global competition is a far more powerful stimulant to innovation than domestic competition. Other cultures have other perspectives, other ways of seeing things. Their ideas bring a richer mix to business thinking. But a higher level of competence and self-esteem is required to play in this arena. We are now operating in a context of constantly escalating challenge—that is the basic point here.

4. *The increasing demands on individuals at every level of a business enterprise—not just at the top but throughout the system—for self-management, personal responsibility, self-direction, a high level of consciousness, and a commitment to innovation and contribution as top priorities.*

The older bureaucratic command-and-control pyramid, modeled after the military, has progressively given way to flatter structures (fewer levels of management), flexible networks, cross-functional teams, and ad hoc combinations of talents coming together for particular projects and then disbanding. The requirements of the flow of knowledge and information are determining organizational structure, rather than preconceived mechanical layers of authority. The ranks of middle managers have been progressively thinned, not merely as a cost-cutting strategy but because computers have taken over the task of relaying information throughout the system, making the role of manager-as-relay-station superfluous.

From the boardroom to the factory floor, work is understood more and more clearly as an expression of thought. As equipment and machinery have become more sophisticated, the knowledge and skill required to operate them has risen accordingly. Employees are expected to monitor them, service them, repair them if necessary, anticipate needs, solve problems—in a word, function as self-respecting, self-responsible professionals. Everyone is expected to think—optimally, not minimally.

From the boardroom to the factory floor, work is now an expression of thought.

5. *The entrepreneurial model and mentality becoming central to our thinking about economic adaptiveness.*

When we think of entrepreneurship, our first association is with independent entrepreneurs who start new businesses or pioneer new industries. And yet today we know that entrepreneurship is essential to the continued success of big business. This was the inescapable lesson of the 1980s.

In the last two decades there has been an explosion of entrepreneurship, almost entirely in small and medium-sized business. By the late 1980s, between 600,000 and 700,000 new enterprises were started every year, as against one-sixth or one-seventh of these figures during the best years of the 1950s and 1960s. While the Fortune 500 companies have been losing workers steadily since the early 1970s, and many of these companies have been struggling for survival, small and medium-sized business was able to create roughly eighteen million new jobs; the majority of these jobs were in firms with fewer than twenty employees. Small and medium-sized businesses have displayed an innovativeness and flexibility—an ability to respond to market changes and opportunities with lightning speed—too often lacking in larger, more cumbersome organizations.

They led the way in showing the path big business must follow if it is to remain competitive. While many companies are still struggling with the problem of balancing traditional administrative management on one hand and entrepreneurial management on the other—the first focused on protecting and nurturing that which already exists, the second on making it obsolete—it is now increasingly obvious that entrepreneurship cannot be the prerogative of small or new businesses. It is imperative all the way up to organizations the size of General Motors—and right now GM is struggling with just this challenge.

Entrepreneurship cannot be the prerogative of small or new businesses.

The essence of entrepreneurial activity is endowing resources with new wealth-producing capabilities—that is, seeing and actualizing productive possibilities that have not been seen and actualized before. This presupposes the ability to think for oneself, to look at the world through one's own eyes—a lack of excessive regard for the-world-as-perceived-by-others—at least in some respects. We are talking about autonomy. And autonomy is intimately linked to self-esteem.

In the context of big business, to become entrepreneurial means to learn to think like small business at its most imaginative and aggressive: to cultivate lightness, lack of encumbrance, swiftness of response, constant alertness to developments that signal new opportunities. This means, among other things, radically reducing bureaucracy and freeing units to operate entrepreneurially.

Low self-esteem correlates with resistance to change and with clinging to the known and familiar. It also correlates with the opposite: the impulsive and erratic embracing of fads (depending on other personality variables). Either way, low self-esteem is economically disadvantageous.

Low self-esteem is economically disadvantageous.

With regard to change that is realistically desirable, if self-esteem correlates with comfort in managing such change and in letting go of yesterday's attachments—and we will see that it does—then high self-esteem confers a competitive edge.

There is an important principle to be identified here. In the early years of American business, when the economy was fairly stable and change relatively slow, the bureaucratic style of organization worked reasonably well. As markets became more turbulent and the pace of change quickened, it became less and less adaptive, unable to respond swiftly to new developments. Relating these facts to the need for self-esteem, we can say that the more stable the economy and the slower the rate of change, the less urgent the need for large numbers of individuals with healthy self-esteem. The more turbulent the economy and the more rapid the rate of change—which is clearly the world of the present and future—the more urgent the need for large numbers of self-esteeming individuals.

6. *The emergence of mind as the central and dominant factor in all economic activity.*

In an agricultural economy, wealth is identified with land. In a manufacturing economy, it is identified with the ability to make things: capital assets and equipment, machines and the various materials used in industrial production. In either of these societies, wealth is understood in terms of matter, not mind; physical assets, not knowledge and information.

In a manufacturing society, intelligence is the guiding force behind economic progress, to be sure, but when people think of wealth, they think of raw materials such as nickel and copper, and physical property such as steel mills and textile looms.

High self-esteem confers a competitive edge.

Wealth is created by transforming the materials of nature to serve human purposes—by transforming a seed into a harvest, by transforming a waterfall into a source of electricity, by transforming iron ore, limestone, and coal into steel, and steel into the girders of apartment buildings. If all wealth is the product of mind and labor, of thought directing action, then one way to understand the transition from an agricultural to a manufacturing economy is to say that the balance between mental and physical effort is profoundly altered. Labor began to move along a declining arc of importance, while mind began to climb.

As an extension of human intelligence, a machine substitutes the power of thought for the power of muscles. While making physical labor less demanding, it makes it more productive. As technological developments keep evolving, the ratio keeps shifting in favor of mind. And as mind becomes more important, self-esteem becomes more important.

The climax of this process of development is the emergence of an information economy in which material resources count for less and less and knowledge and new ideas count for almost everything.

The value of a computer, for instance, lies not in its material constituents but in its design, in the thinking and knowledge it embodies—and in the quantity of human effort it makes unnecessary. Microchips are made out of sand; their value is a function of the intelligence encoded within them. A copper wire can carry forty-eight telephone conversations; a single fiber-optic cable can carry more than eight thousand conversations—yet fiber-optic cables are cheaper, more efficient, and much less energy-consuming to produce than copper.

Each year since 1979 the United States has produced more with less energy than the year before. The worldwide drop in the price of raw materials is a consequence of the ascendancy of mind in our economic life.

A University of Pennsylvania study conducted by Robert Zemsky and Susan Shaman reported the following: a 10 percent rise in worker education resulted in an 8.5 percent rise in productivity; a 10 percent capital expenditure on physical assets resulted in a 3.8 percent rise in productivity.

The mind has always been our basic tool of survival. But for most of our history, this fact was not understood. Today, it is obvious to (almost) the whole world.

Whether you are a CEO or a beginner embarking on your first job, your chief economic strength is your ability to think (integrated, to be sure, with what is now called "emotional intelligence").[5] This understood, let us consider why and how your self-esteem can play a vital role in the kind of life and career you create for yourself.

2

The Dynamics of Self-Esteem

There is no value judgment more important, no factor more decisive in your psychological development and motivation, than the estimate you pass on yourself.

This estimate is ordinarily experienced, not as a conscious, verbalized judgment, but as a feeling—more precisely, an experience—that can be hard to isolate and identify because it is present constantly; it is background to every other experience; it is the basic context or container of all your responses.

This particular self-experience has profound effects on your thinking processes, emotions, desires, values, goals, and ways of interpreting the meaning of events. It is the single most illuminating key to your behavior. If you know in what you invest your self-esteem, and what you do to protect it, and how the level of your self-esteem affects your choices and responses, you have attained a high level of self-understanding.

Self-esteem is the single most illuminating key to your behavior.

To refine and amplify a definition given earlier: *Self-esteem is the disposition to experience yourself as being competent to cope with the basic challenges of life and of being worthy of happiness*. It is made of two components: self-efficacy and self-respect. Self-efficacy is confidence in the efficacy of your mind, in your ability to think; by extension, it is confidence in your ability to learn, make appropriate choices and decisions, and respond effectively to change. Self-respect is the experience that success, achievement, fulfillment—happiness—are right and natural for you. The survival value of such confidence is obvious. So is the danger when it is missing.

I speak of self-esteem as a *disposition* to experience yourself a particular way because when we speak of a person's self-esteem, we mean the average level of that self-esteem. As with all psychological states, there are fluctuations. Further, self-esteem exists on a continuum: no one is entirely lacking in self-esteem and no one is without the capacity to grow in self-esteem; it is always a matter of degree.

Although *self-esteem* is sometimes used interchangeably with *self-image*, the concept runs much deeper than any image. As a particular way of experiencing the self, it is more complex than any mental picture of yourself and more basic than any transitory feeling. It contains cognitive, evaluative, and emotional components—how you see yourself, evaluate yourself, feel about yourself.

In addition, it entails certain action dispositions. When self-esteem is high, the action dispositions are to move toward life rather than away from it, to move toward consciousness rather than away from it, to treat facts with respect rather than denial, to operate self-responsibly rather than irresponsibly. When self-esteem is low, the action dispositions are the opposite.

Self-esteem is not the temporary euphoria or buoyancy of a drug, a compliment, or a love affair. It is not an illusion or hallucination. It is not a shallow feel-good phenomenon. If one does not ground it in reality, does not build it over time through the appropriate operation of mind, it is not self-esteem.[1]

What we tell ourselves about our self-esteem and what it actually is may be quite different. It might please us to believe that our self-esteem is relatively high when in fact it is seriously troubled.

Our life might be unconsciously organized around the attempt to protect a self-esteem we do not possess—what I call a pseudo-self-esteem—perhaps by making ourselves seem right by always making others seem wrong. Nothing is more common than to deny or avoid our fears and self-doubts, thereby preventing them from ever being healed or resolved.

If you are fully willing to confront your self-esteem problems, to face and accept reality, you create the possibility of change and growth. If you deny your problems, you sentence yourself to being stuck in the very pain you wish to escape.

This is not to imply that if only you were willing to face your problems, solutions would always come easily. You might be suffering from blocks you cannot overcome without professional help, or from a lack of the knowledge that could expand your options. Just the same, it is safe to say that how you respond to discomfiting realities reveals a great deal about your deepest vision of who you are—how secure or insecure you feel. It also reveals what kind of future you are likely to shape.

To face life with (reality-based) assurance rather than anxiety and self-doubt is to enjoy an inestimable advantage: your judgments and actions are less likely to be distorted and misguided. A tendency to make irrational decisions, as well as fear of making decisions, are both observable consequences of intellectual self-distrust.

Self-respect tends to inspire respect from others.

To face human relationships with a benevolent, nonarrogant sense of your own value is, again, to enjoy an important advantage: self-respect tends to inspire respect from others. A tendency to form destructive relationships—and to experience the suffering they occasion as your destiny—are familiar effects of feeling unlovable and without value.

The Need for Self-Esteem

Self-esteem is a vitally important psychological need. The root of that need is the fact that our life and well-being depend on the appropriate exercise of mind—and that process is not automatic. It represents an act of choice.

We are not automatically programmed to focus our attention where it is most needed: we are free to look—or look away. We are not automatically programmed to be rational just because rationality is urgently required: we are free to think—or to avoid thinking. We are not automatically programmed to confront and consider facts just because it is in our best interest to do so: we have the option of evasion. We control the switch that turns consciousness brighter or dimmer. As a species we contain within our design a capacity for cognitive self-regulation: that is our free will.

This means that whether we learn to operate mentally in such a way as to make ourselves appropriate to life is ultimately a function of our choices. Do we strive for consciousness or its opposite? For rationality or its opposite? For coherence and clarity or its opposite? For truth or its opposite? And through our choices do we make of ourselves a person we can admire—or the opposite?

No one can be indifferent to the answers to these questions—any more than you can be indifferent to the face looking at you in the mirror.

The Difference It Makes

The level of your self-esteem has profound consequences for every aspect of your existence: how you operate in the workplace, how you deal with people, how high you are likely to rise, how much you are likely to achieve—and, in the personal realm, with whom you are likely to fall in love, how you interact with your spouse, children, and friends, and what level of personal happiness you attain.

The relationship between self-esteem and achievement is not a simple one. It is safe enough to observe that self-esteem makes the path to achievement easier and more likely. And yet a person of troubled self-esteem but high intelligence, a strong achievement orientation, and a tenacious disposition may manage to accomplish a good deal. What will be missing is the ability to enjoy what has been achieved. Nothing ever feels like enough. Often this is the key to understanding a workaholic.

There are significant correlations between healthy self-esteem and a variety of other traits that bear on the capacity for achievement and happiness. Healthy self-esteem correlates with rationality, realism, intuitiveness, creativity, independence, flexibility, ability to manage change, willingness to admit and correct mistakes, benevolence, and cooperativeness. Poor self-esteem correlates with the opposite traits.[2] As we reflect on the meaning of self-esteem and the conditions of its attainment, we see that there is logic to these correlations.

The relationship between the level of your self-esteem and any particular behavior is not a simple, linear, causal one. Your self-esteem simply represents the context that makes certain behavior more or less likely, more or less natural for you.

For example, if you face a difficult problem or challenge from a base of confidence in your mind, chances are you will persevere; persevering, you will not always succeed, but you will succeed more often than you fail; in succeeding, you will reconfirm and reinforce your initial confidence. If you face a difficult problem or challenge from a base of doubt in your mind's ability, chances are at some point you will give up or cease to give your best effort, since you feel in your heart the verdict is already in and it is against you; giving up, or giving much less than your best, you will fail more often than you succeed—and your failure will reconfirm and reinforce your initial self-doubt. Either way, your self-esteem, such as it is, generates a self-fulfilling prophecy.

If you suffer a defeat in your work—the business loses money, the strategy fails, the deal falls through, the customer goes elsewhere, the promotion does not happen—but you face that defeat with a solid self-esteem, you tend to manifest resilience; you pick yourself up and get back in the ring. If you suffer defeat and have an underdeveloped self-esteem, the danger is that you will fall into blaming, alibiing, scapegoating, denial, passivity, depression, or despair.

It is inevitable in the course of any career that sometimes you make mistakes and sometimes you fail. What is decisive for your future is not the defeat but the state of mind with which you greet it. An astonishingly high number of our most successful entrepreneurs have one or more bankruptcies in their past; failure did not stop them.

If you face other human beings with a secure sense of your own value, you tend to convey respect and good will, since self-respect is the base of respect for others. You do not tend to fall into gratuitously adversarial relationships. You are not driven to make yourself big by making someone else small. Benevolence feels natural to you. If you face other human beings with a sense of inadequacy or even worthlessness, you tend to bring fear and hostility into your relationships. Benevolence feels impossible to you. You have no time or energy to really encounter the other person: you are too preoccupied with your own anxieties. If you expect to be disliked or rejected, you may behave in ways that make your expectations come true. If you expect not to be taken seriously, you may behave in ways that guarantee it.

Thus self-esteem is intimately tied to interpersonal competence—and by *competence*, in this context, I mean the ability to deal with other human beings in ways that are satisfying both to you and to them. Since most of our goals and purposes in life, both professional and personal, require at some point the cooperation and participation of other people, this is an ability of no small importance. Its lack is a major source of frustration and disappointment.

If you have good self-esteem, your communications are likely to be open, honest, and appropriate—because you believe your thoughts have value and therefore you welcome rather than fear clarity. If you have poor self-esteem, your communications are likely to be muddy, evasive, and inappropriate—because of uncertainty about your thoughts and feelings or anxiety about the listener's response.

The higher your self-esteem, the more disposed you are to form nourishing rather than toxic relationships. The reason is that like is drawn to like, and health is attracted to health. Vitality and expansiveness are naturally more appealing to persons of good self-esteem than are emptiness, dependency, and insecurity.

We tend to feel most comfortable, most at home, with persons whose level of self-esteem approximates our own. Opposites may attract about some issues, but not about this one. High self-esteem individuals tend to be drawn to high self-esteem individuals. We do not see a passionate love affair between persons at opposite ends of the self-esteem continuum—just as we do not see a passionate romance between intelligence and stupidity: the erotic charge is not there. (I am not saying we might never see a "one-night stand," but that is another matter. I am speaking of passionate love, not a brief infatuation or sexual episode, which can operate by a different set of dynamics). Medium self-esteem individuals are typically attracted to medium self-esteem individuals. Low self-esteem seeks low self-esteem in others—not consciously, to be sure, but by the logic of that which leads us to feel we have encountered a soul mate.

If the greatest barrier to success is the feeling that you are not a person to whom success is possible or appropriate, the greatest barrier to romantic happiness is the feeling that you are not lovable or that you are undeserving of love. You have doubtless heard the observation, "If you do not love yourself, you will be unable to love others." This is true, but there is another aspect, less well understood. If you do not love yourself, it is very difficult to believe or accept that someone else loves you. If you do not accept yourself, how can you accept another's love for you? And in your nonacceptance, you can sabotage your chance for happiness.

One of the advantages of self-esteem is that you do not tend to escalate small frictions into major problems. You are not easily thrown off your center. You are not *touchy*—not overly sensitive. You do not quickly fall into defensiveness or reactive hostility. You tend to focus on solutions, on resolutions, rather than on self-justification. This is a great asset in the workplace—or in marriage.

If degrees of self-esteem are thought of as being on a scale from 1 to 10, with 10 representing optimal self-esteem and 1 representing the lowest level imaginable, then if a manager is a 5, who is he or she more likely to hire, a 7 or a 3? I have posed this question to many executives and the response always is—correctly—a 3. Multiply this example hundreds or thousands of times and project the consequences for a business.

Poor Self-Esteem in the Workplace

Here are a few more examples of how low self-esteem can manifest itself in the arena of work:

> A woman receives a promotion in her company and is swallowed by panic at the thought of not possibly being able to master the new challenges and responsibilities. "I'm an imposter! I don't belong here!" she tells herself. Feeling in advance that she is doomed, she is not motivated to give her best. Unconsciously, she begins a pattern of self-sabotage: coming to meetings unprepared, being harsh with staff one minute and solicitous and placating the next, clowning at inappropriate moments, ignoring signals of dissatisfaction from the boss. When she gets fired she tells herself, "I knew it was too good to be true."

The implicit reasoning here is as follows: If I die by my own hand, at least I am still in control; I spare myself the anxiety of waiting for destruction to come from an outside source. The anxious feeling of being out of control is unbearable; I must end it any way I can.

The head of a research and development lab is informed that the firm has brought in a brilliant scientist from another company. He immediately translates this to mean that his superiors are dissatisfied with his work, in spite of much evidence to the contrary. He imagines the new man will eventually be appointed head of the department. In a fit of blind rebelliousness, he allows his work to deteriorate. When his lapses are pointed out to him, he lashes out defensively—and quits.

When our illusion of self-esteem rests on the fragile support of never being challenged, when our insecurity finds evidence of rejection where no rejection exists, it is only a matter of time until our inner time bomb explodes. The form of the explosion is self-destructive behavior.

A manager reads a superb idea proposed by a subordinate, feels a sinking sense of humiliation that the idea did not occur to her, imagines being overtaken and surpassed by the subordinate—and begins plotting to bury the proposal.

This kind of destructive envy is a product of an impoverished sense of self. Your achievement threatens to expose my emptiness; the world will see—worse, I will see—how insignificant I am. Generosity toward the achievements of others is emblematic of self-esteem.

An auditor from an independent accounting firm meets with the CEO of the client organization. He knows he needs to tell this man some news he will not want to hear. Unconsciously he fantasizes being in the presence of his intimidating father—and stutters and stammers and does not communicate a third of what he had intended. His hunger for the CEO's approval or wish to avoid his disapproval overwhelms his professional judgment. Later, after putting into his written report all the things he should have said to the CEO in person before the report was released, when remedial action might still have been possible, he sits in his office trembling with anxiety, anticipating the CEO's reaction.

When we are moved primarily by fear, sooner or later we precipitate the very calamity we dread. If we fear condemnation, we behave in ways that ultimately elicit disapproval. If we fear anger, eventually we make people angry.

These vignettes could be joined by countless others. But they are sufficient to make the point: low self-esteem is a continuing hazard to our well-being and long-term effectiveness. I want, therefore, to pick up the thread of what healthy self-esteem depends on.

Low self-esteem threatens our well-being and long-term effectiveness.

Childhood

Childhood experiences—or, more precisely, the way a child interprets his or her experiences—tend to lay the foundation for the level of self-esteem that will emerge later in life.

Adults who give a child a rational, noncontradictory impression of reality; who relate lovingly, respectfully, and with belief in a child's competence and worth; who avoid insults, ridicule, and emotional or physical abuse; and who uphold standards and values that inspire the best in a child—such adults can often make the path to healthy self-esteem seem simple and natural (although not invariably or necessarily; a child's own choices and decisions should not be discounted). Adults who deal with a child in the opposite manner can make the path to self-esteem far more difficult and sometimes impossible (without some form of help).

In psychotherapy, work with self-esteem may have to begin with healing childhood psychic wounds, breaking destructive patterns of behavior, dissolving blocks, or neutralizing anxiety. However, although it can clear the ground, the elimination of negatives does not produce self-esteem. Just as the absence of suffering does not equal the presence of happiness, so the absence of anxiety does not equal the presence of confidence. Self-esteem is built over time by specific practices, specific ways of operating in the world.

What nurtures and sustains self-esteem in grown-ups is not how others deal with us but how we ourselves operate in the face of life's challenges—the choices we make and the actions we take.

This leads us to the six pillars of self-esteem.

The Six Pillars

Over four decades of study have led me to identify six practices as the most essential to building self-esteem.

1. *The practice of living consciously:* respect for facts; being present to what you are doing while you are doing it (for example, if your customer, supervisor, employee, supplier, colleague is talking to you, being present to the encounter); seeking and being eagerly open to any information, knowledge, or feedback that bears on your interests, values, goals, and projects; seeking to understand not only the world external to self but also your inner world as well, so that you do not act out of self-blindness.

To work at cultivating the kind of awareness I am describing is a noble pursuit, even a heroic one, because truth is sometimes frightening or painful, and the temptation to close your eyes is sometimes strong.

2. *The practice of self-acceptance:* the willingness to own, experience, and take responsibility for your thoughts, feelings, and actions, without evasion, denial, or disowning—and also without self-repudiation; giving yourself permission to think your thoughts,

experience your emotions, and look at your actions without necessarily liking, endorsing, or condoning them. If you are self-accepting, you do not experience yourself as always on trial, and what this leads to is nondefensiveness and willingness to hear critical feedback or different ideas without becoming hostile and adversarial.

The practice of self-acceptance is the virtue of realism applied to the self. It is your willingness to stand in the presence of your thoughts, feelings, and actions, with an attitude that makes approval or disapproval irrelevant: the desire to be aware.

Obviously you will like and enjoy some expressions of who you are more than others; that is not the issue. What is at issue is whether you can be open to that which you may not like or enjoy.

3. *The practice of self-responsibility:* realizing that we are the authors of our choices and actions; that each one of us is responsible for our own life and well-being and for the attainment of our goals; that if we need the cooperation of other people to achieve our goals, we must offer value in exchange; and that the question is not Who's to blame? but always What needs to be done?

The natural development of a human being is from dependency to independence, from helplessness to increasing efficacy, from nonresponsibility to personal accountability. Self-responsibility is the adult expression of this understanding.

4. *The practice of self-assertiveness:* being authentic in your dealings with others; treating your values and person with decent respect in social contexts; refusing to fake the reality of who you are or what you esteem in order to avoid someone's disapproval; being willing to stand up for yourself and your ideas in appropriate ways in appropriate circumstances.

Self-assertiveness is not about running over widows and orphans to get to the front of the line, or being rude to waiters, or behaving as though no one's needs exist but your own. Self-assertiveness, rationally understood, requires the courage to live your values in reality—to stand up for who you are; not to be so controlled by fear of someone's disapproval that you twist your true self out of recognizable form.

5. *The practice of living purposefully:* identifying your short-term and long-term goals or purposes and the actions needed to attain them, organizing behavior in the service of those goals, monitoring actions to be sure you stay on track—and paying attention to outcome so as to recognize if and when you need to go back to the drawing board.

The practice of living purposefully, as opposed to mentally drifting through life, is essential to any genuine sense of control over your existence. It is your goals and purposes that give your days their focus.

To observe that the practice of living purposefully is essential to fully realized self-esteem should not be understood to mean that the measure of your worth is your external achievements. We admire achievements, in others and in ourselves, and it is natural and appropriate for us to do so. But this is not the same thing as saying that our achievements are the measure or grounds of our self-esteem. The roots of your self-esteem are not your achievements per se but those internally generated practices that make it possible for you to achieve—all the self-esteem virtues discussed here.

Steel industrialist Andrew Carnegie once stated, "You can take away our factories, take away our trade, our avenues of transportation and our money—leave us nothing but our organization—and in four years we would reestablish ourselves." His point was that power lies in the source of wealth, not the wealth; in the cause, not the effect. The same principle applies to the relationship between self-esteem and external achievements.

6. *The practice of personal integrity:* living with congruence between what you know, what you profess, and what you do; telling the truth, honoring commitments, exemplifying in action the values you professes to admire; dealing with others fairly and benevolently. When you betray your values, you betray your mind, and self-esteem is an inevitable casualty.

In every organization there are people whom others trust and people whom they do not trust. There is no mystery about what creates trust. It is a matter of congruence, that is, of integrity.

If integrity is a source of self-esteem, it is also an expression of self-esteem.

Building Self-Esteem

This last point applies to more than the practice of integrity. It applies to all the self-esteem virtues. Between self-esteem and the

The behaviors that generate self-esteem are also expressions of self-esteem.

practices that support it, there is reciprocal causation. This means that the behaviors that generate good self-esteem are also expressions of good self-esteem.

Thus living consciously nurtures and supports self-esteem; and also, the possession of self-esteem inclines you to operate consciously—because you experience your mind as efficacious.

If you practice self-acceptance, you build self-esteem; conversely, self-esteem makes self-acceptance easier—because your value is not in doubt or on trial in your own mind.

If you live self-responsibly, you strengthen your self-esteem; and self-esteem inspires self-responsibility—because passivity, alibiing, drifting, and dependence feel alien to you and inimical.

If you are self-assertive, you grow in self-esteem; and self-esteem drives self-assertiveness—because you refuse to treat your person or your values with disrespect.

If you live purposefully, you nurture self-esteem; and self-esteem expresses itself through that practice—because confidence powers the desire to achieve.

If you operate with integrity, you generate self-esteem; and self-esteem inspires integrity—because a love affair with yourself is not one you are eager to sacrifice.

The point is, causality flows in both directions.

Once you understand these practices, you have the power (at least to some extent) to choose them. The power to choose them is the power to raise the level of your self-esteem from whatever point at which you may be starting and however difficult the project may be in the early stages.

If you want to learn to operate more consciously, you will find it useful, for instance, to ask yourself, What would I do (or do differently) if I brought 5 percent more consciousness to my daily activities? Or to my dealings with other people? Or to the challenges of my job? If I brought 5 percent more consciousness to implementing our mission, rethinking strategy, creating more outlets for individual creativity and innovativeness in our organization—what actions might I take? Are there facts I need to examine that I have been avoiding?

If I operated 5 percent more self-acceptingly, or self-responsibly, or self-assertively, or purposefully, or with greater integrity, what new behaviors might I experiment with? Am I willing to begin now?

If I recognize that if I brought 5 percent more self-esteem to my dealings with people I would treat them more generously, am I willing to do so now? If I know that with more self-esteem, I would better protect the people I manage, could I possibly do so now? If I understand that with higher self-esteem I would face unpleasant facts more straightforwardly, why not choose to do so now?

If healthy self-esteem offers an invaluable context for effective action in the workplace, the converse is also true: learning and practicing effective action in the workplace can be a discipline leading to higher self-esteem. Work can be a vehicle for personal development. With that perspective in mind, let us approach the challenges of creating a high-performance organization.

3

The High Self-Esteem Leader

The primary function of a leader in a business enterprise is to persuasively convey a vision of what the organization is to accomplish, and to inspire and empower all those who work for the organization to make an optimal contribution to the fulfillment of that vision and to experience in doing so that they are acting in alignment with their self-interest.

Thus a leader must be a thinker, an inspirer, and a persuader.

A Leader's Ego

The higher the self-esteem of the leader, the more likely it is that he or she can perform this function successfully. A mind that distrusts itself cannot inspire the best in the minds of others. A person who feels undeserving of achievement and success is unlikely to ignite high aspirations in others. Nor can leaders draw forth the best in others if their primary need, arising from their insecurities, is to prove themselves right and others wrong, in which case their relationship to others is not inspirational but adversarial.

It is a fallacy to say that a great leader should be egoless. A leader needs an ego sufficiently healthy that it does not perceive itself as on trial in every encounter—is not operating out of anxiety and defensiveness—so that the leader is free to be task and results-oriented, not oriented toward self-aggrandizement or self-protection.

A healthy ego asks, What needs to be done? An insecure ego asks, How do I avoid looking bad?

A healthy ego asks, What needs to be done?

A young, newly appointed CEO once hired me to assist him in becoming a better leader. He wanted to know, Is there a way to work on being a good leader? I answered that one of the best ways was by working on one's development as a human being—and, in particular, by working on one's self-esteem, by applying the six pillars to the sphere of work and work relationships.

For example, to be effective a leader must be well aligned with reality—open and available to all facts, knowledge, information, data, feedback that bear on the success of the mission of the organization. Openness to facts, pleasant or unpleasant, goes to the heart of what it means to live consciously—and the practice of living consciously is both a source of self-esteem and an expression of self-esteem.

In the last two or three decades we have seen many examples of once-great companies shrink into anemic versions of their former selves, disappear into mergers, or lose significant market share because their leaders refused to confront the fact that strategies that had once been successful were no longer adaptive to the new realities. They were ruled not by a respect for facts but by their wishes and fears. Rather than respond to clearly apparent changes, they stayed lost in dreams of the good old days. Rather than help their staff to see more clearly, which is a leader's responsibility, they were co-conspirators in organizational blindness.

In this connection, and by way of contrast, it is illuminating to quote from an interview Jack Welch of General Electric gave to *Harvard Business Review* some years ago:[1]

> Good business leaders create a vision, articulate the vision, passionately own the vision, and relentlessly drive

it to completion. Above all else, good leaders are open. They go up, down, and around their organization to reach people. . . . They make a religion out of being accessible. . . .

An insecure ego asks, How do I avoid looking bad?

Real communication takes countless hours of eyeball to eyeball, back and forth. It means more listening than talking. [The process of achieving mutual understanding and consensus] must be absolutely relentless. That's a real challenge for all of us. There's still not enough candor in this company.

[By candor I mean] seeing the world as it is rather than as you wish it were. We've seen over and over again that businesses facing market downturn, tougher competition, and more demanding customers inevitably make forecasts that are much too optimistic. This means they don't take advantage of the opportunities change usually offers. Change . . . isn't something to fear; it's an enormous opportunity to reshuffle the deck, to replay the game. . . .

We've had managers at GE who couldn't change, who kept telling us to leave them alone. They wanted to sit back, to keep things the way they were. And that's just what they did—until they and most of their staffs had to go. That's the lousy part of the job. What's worse is that we still don't understand why so many people are incapable of facing reality, of being candid with themselves and others.

What Welch is stressing here is the importance of what I call a sense of reality—a respect for facts—and the tragedies that result when people resist, avoid, or deny that which clearly, implacably, is.

The first law of self-esteem and the first principle of effective leadership are the same: Thou shalt be aware. Dismissing pertinent realities in the name of short-term comfort is not an acceptable option.

In the professional realm or the personal, any time we choose to confront painful realities that we know need to be addressed—because they bear on our values, goals, and projects—two results follow. Our actions become more appropriate and we grow in self-esteem. We feel more effective because we are more effective.

Leadership begins with the leader possessing a vision to which he or she is passionately committed, a specific and concrete agenda for actualizing that vision, and an unrelenting focus on results. After that, many factors contribute to success or failure. But no factor is more fundamental than the leader's degree of openness to reality, respect for reality, and speed of appropriate response to reality.

Nothing is intrinsically irrational about the impulse to pull back from that which is frightening or painful. All of us have such impulses. But if we have a well-developed sense of reality and a capacity for self-discipline, we recognize that there are circumstances in which it is dangerous to allow fear and pain to have the last word. Sometimes we need to do things that scare us. Sometimes we need to look at things that are painful. If we don't, the consequences will be bad for us. Understanding this, we know that sometimes all we can do is draw a deep breath and proceed.

What kind of factors might obstruct the process of living consciously? Well, for instance:

- Fear of our fallibility
- Fear of taking on new challenges with no guarantee of success
- Fear of facing truths about ourselves (our thoughts,

feelings, or actions) we have been denying and disowning so as to protect our self-esteem or our pretense at it

- Fear of facing truths about another person (a business partner, an associate, or a spouse) that, if acknowledged, might impel us to rock the boat of the relationship or even to destroy it
- Fear of not knowing how to deal with the realities one is acknowledging (very common both in business and in personal life)
- Fear of losing face in the eyes of significant others if certain truths about oneself are brought out into the open, so that one conceals past mistakes rather than correcting them
- Fear of self-responsibility; fear of being held accountable should one's judgment prove to be mistaken

This list is far from exhaustive. I have not mentioned plain laziness or inertia, for instance, or the blindness that can be summoned to obfuscate reluctance to give up power when that is clearly what the situation demands. But I think what I have listed is sufficient in the context.

To anticipate a misunderstanding: I do not mean to imply that if only we confront reality we will always know the right actions to take. There are no guarantees. But what we will do is increase the odds of discovering the right actions.

An Exercise in Waking Up

If we are mentally blocked and unable to see our way clearly in some area, what can we to do shift to a higher and more powerful level of consciousness? One of my most effective techniques, originating in my work as a psychotherapist and then applied to corporate consulting, is the sentence-completion process. Here are two examples of how it can work.

The CEO of an accounting firm raised a problem he described as acutely embarrassing. He said that his business was growing fast and that he needed to hire a brilliant, high-level executive—in effect, a number two person—but that he was afraid of hiring someone cleverer than himself. I complimented him on his honesty and suggested that rather than work the problem out in my office, I preferred to provide him with a means of solving it himself.

Each morning for two weeks, I explained, at the start of his business day he was to open a confidential notebook and write this incomplete sentence at the top of a fresh page: *"If I bring 5 percent more consciousness to my fear of hiring a brilliant executive—"* Then, as quickly as his pen could move over paper, without editing, censoring, or taking time to think, he was to write six to ten endings for that sentence stem. He was to repeat this process every day, without reading his work from the day before. Naturally there would be some repetitions but he was not to worry about that; new material inevitably would emerge. In two weeks we would meet again to review the situation.

Sentence-completion work is a deceptively simple yet powerful tool for expanding self-awareness, self-understanding, and personal growth. There is almost no limit to the kinds of problems it can address. If done properly, without self-criticism while one is doing it—and with invention if one gets stuck, to keep the flow unobstructed—the technique triggers spontaneous insights and integrations and connects a person with knowledge and wisdom never made explicit or articulate but residing in the psyche beneath awareness.

"Problem solved," were my client's first words when he triumphantly entered my office at our next meeting. It was as if, he announced, he had "radiated" his problem with such a high intensity of awareness that he could see through his fears, see their foolish irrelevance, see that by failing to seek out the most brilliant person he could find he was acting against his own interests. At the end of the first week of the program, he said, "the fears and the procrastination felt silly."

He volunteered that his sentence completions included such endings as:

"—I'd see that the smarter the person I hire, the better off I'll be."

"—I'd see that my fear is an old reaction no longer relevant."

"—I'd recognize how much I love and admire competence."

"—I'd recognize how starved I am for brains."

"—I'd see I have to update my self-concept because this fear is stupid."

"—this reaction really feels unworthy of me and I no longer can even hold on to the perspective from which it came."

The sentence-completion technique is not the only way this problem could have been solved, but I chose it because I wanted my client to experience his own resourcefulness, not mine. I wanted the method of solving it to be self-esteem-enhancing for him.

On another occasion, working face to face in my office, I asked him to do a series of completions for the sentence stem *"If I bring 5 percent more awareness to the challenges of being an effective leader—"* His endings included:

"—I see that if I play the Lone Ranger, my people are going to feel abandoned by and cut off from me."

"—it's obvious that if I want their best, I've got to create more of a relationship with them."

"—I've got to drop the notion that the only good ideas are mine."

"—I'll control my impatience and listen—whether their suggestions and proposals always seem good to me or not."

"—I'll see that if I really want people's creative participation, I've got to learn to keep my ears open and my mouth shut even when it's hard as hell to do."

"—I'll face that it's not enough that I think my people are great, I've got to let them know it, and not just with money but also with respect."

What is noteworthy is that we had never discussed leadership before this day and to the best of my knowledge he had never read a book on the subject. Yet at some level he knew a good deal about it, which he did not know he knew; that was my starting premise. The first assignment, therefore, was to make his awareness explicit.

With a little coaching he learned to make himself a more effective leader while strengthening his self-esteem by bringing his behavior into alignment with his knowledge.

Trust

If integrity is one of the cardinal pillars of self-esteem, it is an equally essential pillar of effective leadership. The reason is the intimate relationship that exists between integrity and the ability to inspire trust.

Studies of leadership—not only in business organizations but also in the military—clearly show that whereas people can and will perform extraordinary feats for leaders whom they trust, their performance tends to be less impressive when that trust is lacking.

It is no mystery how trust is created. It is a matter of congruence between words and actions. To reduce this issue to its simplest fundamentals:

One tells the truth. One keeps promises. One honors commitments. One's behavior manifests one's professed values. One deals with people fairly and justly.

I once sat with a group of vice presidents at a major brokerage house who were complaining that there was a lack of trust in their organization and were wondering how to correct the situation. I asked them to write down the sentence stem "*If I want to be perceived as trustworthy*—" and then write six to ten endings. Then they all read their completed sentences aloud. There were no surprises and no significant differences of opinion, merely some differences of emphasis. Everyone knew what needed to be done. Here is the essence of what they came up with:

- Tell the truth and make it safe for others to do so.
- Keep promises.
- Walk your talk.
- Don't just preach "respect for each individual"—exemplify it in your behavior.
- Manifest integrity and communicate that nothing less is acceptable.
- Understand that meeting your numbers is not enough; you must also live your professed values (assuming those values include honesty and integrity).
- Set an example.
- Exemplify fairness and even-handedness in all your dealings with people.

When it comes to setting an example, ultimate responsibility necessarily falls on the leader. Unfortunately, few company heads understand or appreciate the extent to which they are role models. They do not realize how closely their smallest moves are noted and absorbed by those around them, not necessarily consciously, and reflected via those they influence throughout the organization. If a leader is perceived to have integrity, a standard is set that others tend to feel drawn to follow. A leader who treats people with respect—associates, subordinates, customers, suppliers, shareholders—sends a signal of incalculable power, a signal for which no speech or mission statement is a substitute. And conversely, a leader who feels no need to operate with integrity or to be fair and decent in dealings with others also sends a signal that cannot be neutralized by the expression of noble sentiments.

Trust is inspired by consistency and predictability. If we feel we do not know what a leader might do in any particular situation, we cannot feel trust. If someone is sometimes honest and sometimes not, sometimes fair and sometimes not, sometimes values-driven and sometimes not, we may still be able to appreciate that person's other assets—such as intelligence, energy, enthusiasm, creativity—but we will not feel trust. And when we do not trust, we rarely give our best.

I was once asked to consult with a company that was one of the three largest in its industry. The CEO was greatly admired for her energy, innovativeness, willingness to share power—and generosity. Her generosity, however, was deeply impulsive and this created

Few company heads understand or appreciate the extent to which they are role models.

problems in the organization, including the undermining of trust. If she took a personal liking to some employee, or was impressed by something the employee had done, she would often bestow an immense bonus that bore no relationship to the official reward system of the organization. Senior managers constantly had to deal with the problems of resentment that were ignited by the CEO's behavior. The CEO was perceived as not walking the talk, not remaining consistent with the system of rewards that she (her organization) proclaimed. Because of her extraordinary generosity, she had difficulty understanding why people could feel her dealings lacked fairness—lacked integrity.

To say it once more: trust requires consistency and predictability.

Leadership needs more than an inspiring vision. It needs the passion and enthusiasm to translate that vision into real-world results. For this it needs the passion and enthusiasm of other people. Leaders need to enroll others in the vision and its realization. They need to inspire commitment. They cannot do this if they cannot first inspire trust. They do not need to win love, but they do need to win respect—and better still would be to win admiration. This is more likely to be achieved by leaders who have first earned their own esteem.

A great deal of business activity consists essentially of conversations—conversations between representatives of different institutions, conversations between CEOs and their executives, conversations between managers and the people reporting to them, conversations between salespersons and customers, conversations between purchasing specialists and suppliers, conversations between company negotiators and union representatives. All such conversations entail the understanding that people are accountable for what they say, including what they promise to do, and only to the extent that such understanding is honored is business activity possible.

If we understand this, we see that integrity, trust, and character are not peripheral to business but fundamental—which means that self-esteem is fundamental. While this truth is relevant at every level for the long-term success of an enterprise, nowhere does it more urgently need to be kept in constant focus than in the office of the CEO, whose job is to set the standard. CEOs may not usually think of themselves as moral teachers, exemplars, or inspirers—but they are and they should.

During the 1980s, while he was CEO of Chrysler, Lee Iacocca persuaded the union to make major financial concessions on the grounds that the company was caught in hard times. Then Iacocca turned around and gave himself a gigantic bonus. What signal was he sending to Chrysler employees? Was it a signal to inspire higher levels of moral behavior or lower levels? Did Iacocca raise the level of trust or the level of cynicism? Predictably, the next time the union sat down at the bargaining table its representatives were ruthlessly unrelenting in their demands and conceded not an inch; all spirit of cooperation was gone.

Apart from the general matter of integrity, one of the ways leaders generate trust is through the clarity of their communications. Do they articulate clearly not only the general vision but also a concept of how that vision is to be actualized? Do they articulate clearly what they are asking for and requiring from their people—and the ethical and philosophical principles they expect to guide the work—and the nature of the culture they see as the necessary context for their achievements? For example, when Larry Bossidy became CEO of AlliedSignal, he helped design a personal development program and put eighty-six thousand employees through it. But also, during his first year, he personally spoke to fifteen thousand people, explaining his vision, helping them to understand markets and market conditions, lecturing, asking questions, arguing, debating, relentlessly pursuing a shared clarity of understanding concerning what AlliedSignal was to achieve. Over a period of six years, he helped increase the market value of his company by 400 percent. He understood that leaders are teachers and that their first obligation is to be clear.

Yet another way leaders inspire trust (and demonstrate integrity) is by the quality of the people with whom they surround themselves. A leader who seeks out the best, most innovative and independent minds to be found, minds who will not be afraid to disagree with the boss and will not be penalized for doing so—and who makes it abundantly clear that their contributions are welcome—sends a strong signal that will reverberate through the entire organization that the focus is not on "Who's right?" but on "What's right?" It is a signal summoning the best in everyone, and thus tends to attract those who have a decent level of self-esteem, which every organization needs, and also to speak to the spark of self-esteem that exists in almost all human beings. Here again we encounter the strong reality-orientation of which I spoke earlier: not inappropriate self-aggrandizement, not turf-protection, not a battle of personalities, but rather a concern with What's true? What needs to be done? What best serves our mission and our values? Not rank but reality is given the last word. And when a leader embodies this principle we are witnessing not selflessness, self-abnegation, or "absence of ego" but self-esteem in action.

When this reality-orientation is perceived to be consistent and basic to an organization's culture—because a leader exemplifies it, teaches it, insists on it, rewards it (and punishes its opposite)—people feel safe, they feel honored, and they feel trust. And then they may astonish themselves and others with what they are able to accomplish.

One of the secrets of Motorola's extraordinary success is that it rewards employees who successfully challenge faulty premises propounded by senior management. I recall an incident recounted to me by James O'Toole some years ago, when he witnessed an engineer at Motorola publicly disagreeing with then-CEO Robert Galvin and promising to shoot his idea down. When Galvin gave his laughing approval and saw that O'Toole was astonished by it—O'Toole thought that almost anywhere else the engineer would be thrown out or at least be reprimanded—Galvin said, "Are you kidding? This is how we beat the Japanese." That is self-esteem made visible in company policy. Think of the level of trust that would already have to exist at Motorola for the engineer to speak so freely. Small wonder that when one thinks of the most admired and innovative companies today, Motorola always figures prominently.

Aloneness, Decisiveness, and Self-Management

Someone observed that if Moses went up the mountain with a committee, he never would have come back. To be out in front means sometimes to be alone. A leader must understand and accept this responsibility.

If Moses went up the mountain with a committee, he never would have come back.

While full consensus is the ideal, it may not always be realizable, not even by a superb teacher and persuader. To invite everyone's feedback does not mean that everyone has equal authority regarding the final decision. As Max DePree, former chairman of Herman Miller, points out, "Participative management is not democratic. Having a say differs from having a vote."[2] After all the respectful talking, listening, debating, and interacting is done, someone has to say, "This is what we are going to do." That is a leader's job.

The ability of leaders to do this job rests on at least two factors. The first, obviously, is trust in their own ability to think, choose, and make appropriate decisions. The second is their ability to manage any desires they may have to be liked or approved that obstruct the perception of what needs to be done or the will to do it.

The desire to be liked is not abnormal—who would not prefer being liked to being disliked?—although it is true that for some people it is not a desire but an obsession. In any event, the challenge is to avoid being manipulated by that desire in ways that do not serve your long-term interests—for example, making the popular or easy choice rather than the right one.

No leader can be effective who has not learned to manage emotions—whether the emotions pertain to a hunger for popularity, inappropriate exhibitionistic impulses, competitiveness with subordinates, defensiveness, anger, or fear and insecurity. Emotions need to be recognized, owned, experienced, and accepted (non-self-punitively)—but not acted on when to do so conflicts with more important agendas. A leader's job is to guide the organization to the fulfillment of its mission, and not to indulge in personal catharsis at the expense of this primary commitment.

Emotions need to be recognized, owned, experienced, and accepted—but not necessarily acted upon.

The leader's job is to do what he or she honestly thinks is right for the organization. Sometimes this task will test self-esteem. But if, without repression, denial, or disowning, leaders learn to manage and rise above feelings and emotions that may stand in the way—if they place their firsthand judgment of the realities confronting them above all other considerations—they grow in personal stature, grow in self-esteem, as they grow in professional effectiveness. Such a leader becomes a better person and a better executive at the same time and through the same process.

But the ability to operate in this manner presupposes a reasonable level of self-awareness. You cannot successfully manage feelings of which you are ignorant or which you have denied and disowned. On the contrary, such repressed feelings tend to manage you.

Self-awareness (an aspect of living consciously) is one of the characteristics of effective leaders.[3] Without it, they cannot manage themselves; unable to manage themselves, they cannot properly manage others. They will tend to lack the emotional intelligence that is the foundation of interpersonal competence. Without a commitment to self-examination, a leader operates at a severe disadvantage.

The willingness to look at yourself dispassionately, at your thoughts, feelings, and actions—moved by the desire not to judge or condemn but to be aware, learn, and understand—is both a process that strengthens self-esteem and also one that expresses self-esteem. Of course, the need to do so, and the advantage of doing so, is not confined to leaders.

If you know what your weaknesses are, you can learn to compensate for them.

Focusing only on your strengths and being blind to your weaknesses does not strengthen self-esteem. You need to be aware of both. No one is equally strong in all respects; if you know what your weaknesses are, you can learn to compensate for them—which is precisely what effective leaders do. Ineffective leaders do not see themselves realistically, do not recognize that they have any shortcomings, and therefore do not think their way through to solutions—they merely resort to denial, blaming, and alibiing.

Challenges of Leadership

It takes a significant measure of self-esteem to generate a vision that is rational, uplifting, and involves stepping into the unknown—and persuading others to follow one there.

It takes a significant measure of self-esteem to embody and uphold a standard of integrity with such unswerving consistency (regardless of the latest crisis) that it becomes the trademark of an entire organization—thereby creating an internal culture of trust and mutual regard.

It takes a significant measure of self-esteem to give away power, to welcome and embrace the talents of others, never to steal their responsibilities, and to be relentless in communicating one's belief in their potential.

It takes a significant measure of self-esteem to see oneself—assets and limitations—realistically, and to think strategically about how to transcend shortcomings.

Rarely are such things done easily. They demand courage, energy, perseverance, and commitment.

One of the greatest challenges to everyone's self-esteem is that of responding appropriately to change. I will touch on this only briefly here from the leader's perspective, and discuss it in more detail later as an organizational issue.

A great deal is written these days about the problems of leading people in a company through the trauma and anxiety of change—as if leaders do not have to confront the same fear and resistance within themselves. The truth is that change can be a problem for leaders no less than for followers. And the difficulties with change experienced by employees are often the reflection of difficulties existing in the minds of senior management—or the CEO.

I was consulting with the head of an engineering company who complained that his senior executives simply could not understand the philosophy of "the new management"—respect for the individual, treating people as resources rather than costs, talking less and listening more, building consensus rather than flinging orders, making the needs of the customer central, and the like. This man had taken over the firm from a highly autocratic father who had made it into a hugely successful enterprise earlier in the century. While the new president had read all the right books and said all the right things to his people, in his heart he was still attached to his father's style of management, still felt that nothing was as practical as command-and-control, in spite of evidence that changes in the company's policies and structure were needed. When his true feelings finally surfaced with inescapable clarity in one of our meetings, he sighed and acknowledged, "I'm not sure I want a lot of people with self-esteem working for me. I know it sounds ridiculous in today's environment but I want people who know how to take orders and not make a fuss."

This, of course, is why he could not convince his associates: in spite of his fine proclamations, he was not convinced himself.

At some level people know whether the boss means it or not. His senior associates know it and his ambivalence commonly becomes their ambivalence, and their ambivalence travels through the organization like a virus, affecting everyone.

The change this man's intelligence told him was needed in his organization had to happen first in his own mind. This is one of the most important things to understand about leadership.

Was this a self-esteem problem? I would say so, at least in part. He lacked the confidence to move beyond his father's vision of things. He was overattached to the security of the familiar.

When we agreed on this analysis of the problem, I gave him a sentence completion exercise to do, which began with writing six to ten endings for the stem *"If I bring 5 percent more self-esteem to this problem [his resistance to necessary change]—"* His endings were as follows:

"—I would focus on the present and the future, not on memories of father's successes."

"—I would accept how much the world has changed."

"—I would produce a specific agenda to achieving change, not just talk in generalities."

"—I would talk to our people, I would listen to their fears, I would let them air their concerns, I would explain, and talk and talk and talk until I saw that they really got it."

"—I would pull this whole issue out of the clouds and make it a crusade."

"—I would admit how much I see and understand but often ignore and don't use."

"—I'd admit how much I would love to start a new tradition here and not just follow in father's."

"—I'd confront my passivity and conquer it."

"—I'd pay more attention to the excitement I feel when I actually think of doing this."

"—I would not allow myself to be ruled by fear, nostalgia, and inertia; I would shake loose and become my own man, even if it's difficult."

When working with senior executives who are concerned about some problem in their organization, I generally find it useful to explore whether in some form that problem operates inside themselves, as it did in the case of this CEO. More often than not, problems in an organization reflect attitudes and problems at the most senior level and need to be addressed at that level if they are to be resolved. A relatively small amount of corrective action at the top can produce major changes down the line.

Where the Buck Stops

It is here, however, that one encounters a common corporate problem: resistance at the top to taking appropriate responsibility for errors and failures on the part of employees throughout the organization. It is easier to moan, "What's wrong with people?" than to examine where within an organization the problem actually begins.

A few years ago I was asked by a firm that employed about two thousand people to work with "the lower one thousand" in creating a culture of self-responsibility and accountability. I said I would need to begin not with the lower one thousand but with the much smaller number of the most senior executives, explaining that if I could not enroll them in the project, could not win their enthusiasm and support, there was no way to make the undertaking successful. The CEO declined; he did not wish to get involved; he saw it as a problem of "the troops." That alone told me why his company was having problems. In any organization, personal responsibility and accountability—and culture change—begin at the top.

The most effective leaders operate at a high level of self-responsibility. They do not waste energy on blaming. They do not pass the buck. They ask, "Did we err in placing that person in that position? Did we fail to provide the necessary training? Where was the mistake made and how can it be corrected? Is there something I ought to have done differently?"

Here is an admirable example of what I mean. At the time of which I write, Scandinavian Airlines was commonly regarded as one of the best airlines in the world. It was deeply committed to empowering its people, who were encouraged to solve a great many problems on their own authority and without consulting higher-ups. When asked why he did not punish some employees who made errors in the execution of their duties, Jan Carlzon, who was then CEO of SAS, said with astonishment, "Punish them? Why should we have punished them when it was our fault? We believe the task of leaders in a large company is to articulate the values of the organization, to create a system in which people can be productive, and to explain the goals that the system was to achieve. We also believe that people don't act maliciously. If we in top management had done those jobs properly—if we had explained adequately the purpose behind employee empowerment—those few errors would not have occurred. That is why we went back to evaluate our own communication skills."[4]

Such a leadership practice of self-responsibility, openness to self-examination, and commitment to taking corrective action is at once a test of self-esteem, a source of strengthening self-esteem, and also an expression of self-esteem.

A Paradox but Not a Contradiction

There is a paradox in one of the challenges of leadership. On one hand, effective leaders need confidence in their own judgment, perseverance in their vision even when others do not yet share it, ability to tolerate misunderstanding, opposition, and aloneness, and a passion to fulfill that vision that overcomes difficult obstacles. On the other hand, they need the realism to recognize that sometimes they can be wrong, that they become stronger, not weaker, by testing their ideas against the ideas of others, by being open to discovering errors in their thinking and being eager to correct them, and by being fully as much the student and learner as the teacher.

The two attitudes represent only a paradox, not a contradiction, because there is nothing contradictory between confidence in one's judgment and awareness of one's fallibility. A self-esteeming mind can easily and comfortably hold these attitudes in appropriate balance. To be open to new information that may require a revision of some of my premises does not mean that I wander around in uncertainty and self-doubt. It is defensiveness, not openness, that reveals insecurity.

On Not Stealing Responsibilities

The president of a packaging firm came to me with this problem. She had eight managers who reported to her, all "good people," but they had one seemingly intractable failing. When it came to follow-through on their agreements and commitments, they rarely averaged better than 90 percent. The president needed 100 percent and did not know how to get it—having explained, reproached, dialogued, listened, and gotten nowhere. She wondered if perhaps I could provide a solution.

It is defensiveness, not openness, that reveals insecurity.

I explained that my philosophy was that, whenever possible, problems should be solved by the people who created them. I therefore proposed the following experiment.

She was to ask her managers to clear an entire Friday afternoon and meet her in the conference room at one o'clock. When they were assembled she would explain that this afternoon they were to engage in an exercise—call it a kind of game—the purpose of which would shortly be obvious but that nonetheless was to be treated with full seriousness. Here were the instructions she was to give:

"First, find a partner and sit with him or her. Imagine that you are the president of a company more or less like ours. Imagine that you have eight managers who report to you, all terrific people, who have one shortcoming: their follow-through is only 90 percent and you absolutely need 100 percent. Now as it happens the person sitting with you is also the president of a company similar to yours and has the identical problem with eight other managers. So for the next forty-five minutes you two are to brainstorm together, thinking up ways this problem can be solved. Make a list of your best ideas. At the end of forty-five minutes, each dyad joins another dyad, and you compare your lists. For the next forty-five minutes, work together on developing one improved list that integrates your best ideas. At the end of this period, the two groups of four join and compare their lists. Then, prepare one master list that will represent the best ideas of all of you. Take forty-five minutes for this. Everything clear? Good. I'll see you later."

Two weeks later she conducted the experiment. Predictably her staff came up with many more and much better ideas than she or I might have produced in my office. And there was the added advantage that they had done it themselves. They were then instructed to develop an action agenda for translating their ideas in practice.

Virtually immediately the problem of the missing 10 percent disappeared. However, a few months later, two of the eight managers resigned, saying, in effect, that while they understood the necessity of working at this level, they were not comfortable with it. Two new managers who understood what was expected from the beginning and therefore adapted more readily replaced them.

A brilliant leader is someone who inspires others to produce the brilliant solutions.

The moral of the story? A brilliant leader is not someone who produces brilliant solutions. It is someone who inspires other people to produce the brilliant solutions.

Operating Under Pressure

There is a phenomenon commonly encountered in the practice of psychotherapy that has an exact analogue in the world of business.

One of the tasks of a psychotherapist is teaching new skills or new ways of functioning that better serve the interests of the client than those previously employed. For example, suppose a client has never learned to air a grievance or utter a complaint without explosive anger accompanied by attacks on the psychology or morality of the listener. Obviously such a style of communication invites defensiveness and serves only to escalate conflict. So the client is taught to describe the disturbing event, the feelings it evokes, and, when appropriate, describe what action he or she would like taken—and to omit character assassination in the process. A client might be taught to say, "When you make plans involving both of us without consulting me, and then become impatient if I object, I feel unvalued and discounted—and not especially inclined to accommodate you. If you want my cooperation, you're going to need to ask me in advance of your making commitments for both us." This is instead of, "You're the most uncaring and inconsiderate human being I've ever known! You make plans and you don't give a damn what works or doesn't work for me! You're an egomaniac who never gives anyone but yourself a thought about anything! You're completely narcissistic!"

Over time the client sees that the first style of communication produces more satisfying results than the second, sees that the listener is more open to hearing, is less likely to launch into a counterattack, more likely to stay focused on the important issue—namely, the need to discuss plans in advance of making commitments. The listener is not sidetracked and distracted by wondering whether the charge of narcissism is true, is not flung into defensiveness, self-protection, and self-justification, all of which are irrelevant. At first, this new way of talking no doubt feels like a foreign language, but slowly it feels more natural—until one day when the client becomes much more upset over something than usual, forgets all the new learnings, and starts screaming and attacking in the old style.

This tends to happen, until a new habit is thoroughly internalized and automatized, because under pressure we tend to regress to older, more primitive modes of reaction. The stronger our self-esteem, the less likely this regression is to happen, because the ego is better able to handle pressure without disintegration—but the point is, for most people such regression is a common occurrence.

The analogy to business is this: When things are going well and profits are rising, leaders may find it easy to practice the kind of principles discussed in this chapter. They may win laurels in *Fortune* magazine or in business books for being enlightened. Then, when business takes a downturn, competition intensifies, interest rates rise, stock prices fall, or market share begins to shrink for any number of reasons, leaders may forget all this "soft stuff" such as treating individuals with respect, may become less concerned with ethics in their dealings with customers, less willing to tolerate dissent, or more autocratic in their overall manner of functioning—because they are frightened and because their anxiety has flung them back to earlier, less adaptive forms of behavior. Their ego-strength was not sufficient to withstand the pressure of the new difficulties and challenges.

Leaders who succumb do not tell themselves their driving motive is fear. They tell themselves their behavior reflects the fact that "the times demand toughness." But since their notion of toughness is not the answer, and since they abandoned the better policies when they most needed them, their business problems tend only to become exacerbated. Of the various causes of business failure during the 1980s, this was one clearly maladaptive pattern.

This is one explanation (of course not the only one) for the oft-noted phenomenon of a company being hailed by business writers as enlightened only to fall on troubled times some years later and vanish from these writers' lists. When times got tough, these companies stopped doing the things that qualified them for "enlightened" status and collapsed back into the category of the reactionary. They did not persist in the virtues that had made them successful—exactly like therapy clients who abandon the new learnings that had improved their quality of life.

Training Leaders

If there is one aspect of successful leadership that the modern U.S. military seems to understand better than anyone, it is the importance of a leader training others to be leaders.

In war, if a leader is incapacitated or killed in battle, someone else steps forward instantly to take his place and assume the leadership. And should he fall, there will be another man in line to step forward. Students of the Normandy invasion invariably comment on this phenomenon and the victory that it helped make possible. The ability of leaders to be replaced is a battlefield imperative and officers are evaluated for their competence in training others for leadership roles. This is understood to be one of their essential duties. An insecure but ambitious officer may be eager to hoard his power and establish himself as irreplaceable, but he knows the army will judge him accordingly—as a failure in at least one crucial respect. If he chooses to indulge his psychological problems, he very likely pays a price.

Warren Bennis once remarked to me, "I learned more about leadership in four months of officer training in Fort Benning, Georgia, than I learned anywhere in the rest of my career. When it comes to knowing how to create leaders, the U.S. military is ahead of everyone. Granted the context of the military is vastly different from that of a private corporation, and not all practices are transferable, still there's a great deal the business community can learn."

There are three basic leadership priorities and everyone in the army is trained in them:

- Accomplish the mission.
- Take care of personnel. (For example, an officer sees that his soldiers are fed and sheltered before attending to his own needs.)
- Create new leaders.

These three priorities are deeply ingrained in military culture to an extent that appears to have no analogue in the modern business corporation. Yet its desirability there seems inescapably obvious. The evidence is clear that the long-term success of a business enterprise requires that it have more leaders at more levels than its competitors. This means that a commitment to creating as many leaders as possible throughout one's organization is a strategic imperative.

Leaders who are secure in the knowledge of their own value are more likely to nurture and support potential leaders rather than feel threatened by them, and to realize that no organization can sustain success without them. The virtue involved is not selflessness but realism—responsibility toward what the situation requires.

For long-term success, a business must have more leaders at more levels than its competitors.

The more a leader's self-esteem is equal to this challenge, the more likely it is that the challenge will be met appropriately—especially since, as I have noted, there is not the same pressure in the business world to do so as there is in the military. As things stand at present, in the world of business self-motivation will have to occupy a higher role.

Up to this point I have principally talked about leaders as CEOs or presidents of corporations. However, within a corporation there are many potential leadership roles. In a corporation the size of IBM or GM there are thousands of spots for leaders who are willing and able to rise to the occasion. Whoever, on any level, takes responsibility for the success of a task and mobilizes others around what needs to be done is operating as a leader. Such men and women are the spark plugs without which no organization can sustain high performance.

This leads us to the question of how one creates a culture in which such leaders are likely to arise—or, more broadly, how one manages work in such a way as to get the best of human brainpower. That is the issue to which we now turn.

4

High Self-Esteem Management

Management of human activity was a good deal less demanding when work was primarily physical. Work was broken down into separate tasks, each task had a job description, and different departments handled different sets of tasks, with each department having its own clearly defined goal. Most of the tasks were simple, mechanical, repetitive, and—assuming a basic level of competence on the part of the manager—relatively easily managed (although perhaps management has never been *easy*—witness John D. Rockefeller's statement that he would pay more for the ability to manage people than for any other talent).

In contrast, knowledge work rarely if ever lends itself to the Frederick Taylor style of task breakdown into simple component parts. It rarely if ever lends itself to the simple and rigid job descriptions that characterize muscle work. It does not consist of repetitive actions. Instead it entails a continuous dialogue with changing data, new information, and colleagues whose work intimately relates to one's own, since virtually everyone is a specialist addressing only one aspect of the total project and (most likely) working not in isolation but rather as a member of a team.

With regard to his or her own specialty, each employee knows more than the manager or supervisor. Therefore, independence, self-responsibility, and some measure of creativity are not merely expected of everyone, they are mandatory. There is no other way for the system to work. However, the concept of "managing" creativity is a dubious one. It is less accurate to say that one manages minds than that one aims them.

The older bureaucratic command-and-control pyramid has progressively given way to flatter structures, flexible networks, cross-functional teams, and ad hoc combinations of talents coming together for particular projects and then disbanding. The requirements of the flow of knowledge and information are determining organization, rather than preconceived mechanical layers of authority. This implies an entirely new concept of human relationships in the workplace, with knowledge and competence replacing rank as the voice of authority.

Knowledge and competence are replacing rank as the voice of authority.

Without the old familiar chains of command, many managers are going through what might be termed a self-esteem crisis: with lines of authority and power no longer clear-cut, they are challenged to find new definitions of their roles, as coach, as facilitator, as support system, rather than as boss. Their need now is to disengage feelings of self-worth from traditional forms of status or from the performance of particular tasks, and to base it instead on their ability to think, to learn, to master new ways of functioning, and to respond appropriately to new realities.

Every change demanding new and unfamiliar responses is a challenge to one's self-esteem. To inspire and facilitate the resourcefulness of others, as their new role demands, managers must first find that resourcefulness within themselves. This means that to be effective they must be willing to confront themselves and work on themselves, work on their personal development, work on their self-esteem. A self-esteem anchored in trust in your mind and its operations is infinitely more reliable than one anchored merely in your status or possession of a particular set of skills.

Bringing Out the Best in People

Today companies have no more important challenge than that of attracting and keeping high-quality people. Right now there is a bad shortage of brains. A business culture that supports and nurtures self-esteem is far more likely to hold bright, talented people than one that does the opposite. Further, an organization whose employees operate at a high level of consciousness, self-acceptance (and acceptance of others), self-responsibility, self-assertiveness (and respect for the assertiveness of others), purposefulness, and personal integrity would be an organization of extraordinarily empowered human beings.

So, as a preliminary sketch of what high self-esteem management might look like, we can observe that the traits just mentioned, "the six pillars," are supported in an organization to the extent that the following conditions are met:

- *People feel safe:* secure that they will not be ridiculed, demeaned, humiliated, or punished for openness and honesty or for admitting "I made a mistake" or for saying "I don't know but I'll find out."
- *People feel accepted:* treated with courtesy, listened to, invited to express thoughts and feelings, dealt with as individuals whose dignity is important—treated, in effect, as volunteers.
- *People feel challenged:* given assignments that excite, inspire, and test and stretch their abilities.
- *People feel recognized:* acknowledged for individual talents and achievements, and rewarded monetarily and nonmonetarily for extraordinary contributions.

- *People receive constructive feedback:* they hear how to improve performance in nondemeaning ways that stress positives rather than negatives and that build on their strengths.
- *People see that innovation is expected of them:* their opinions are solicited, their brainstorming is invited, and they see that the development of new and usable ideas is desired of them and welcomed.
- *People have easy access to information:* not only are they given the information (and resources) they need to do their job properly, they are given information about the wider context of their work—the goals and progress of the company—so that they understand how their activities relate to the organization's overall mission.
- *People have authority appropriate to what they are accountable for:* they are encouraged to take initiative, make decisions, exercise judgment.
- *People work with clear-cut and noncontradictory rules and guidelines:* they are provided with a structure their intelligence can grasp and count on and they know what is expected of them.
- *People are encouraged (perhaps required) to solve as many of their own problems as possible:* they are expected to resolve issues close to the action rather than pass responsibility for solutions to higher-ups, and they are empowered to do so—without power it is meaningless to talk about responsibility.
- *People see that their rewards for successes are far greater than any penalties for failures:* in too many companies, where the penalties for mistakes are much greater than

the rewards for success, people are afraid to take risks or express themselves.

- *People are encouraged and rewarded for learning:* they are encouraged to participate in internal and external courses and programs that will expand their knowledge and skills.
- *People experience congruence between an organization's professed philosophy and the behavior of its leaders and managers:* they see integrity exemplified and they feel motivated to match what they see.
- *People experience being treated fairly and justly:* they feel their workplace is a rational world they can trust.
- *People are able to believe in and take pride in the value of what they produce:* they perceive the result of their efforts as genuinely useful, and they perceive their work as worth doing.

To the extent that these conditions are operative in an organization, it will be a place in which people with high self-esteem will want to work. It will also be one in which people of more modest self-esteem will find their self-esteem raised.

The conditions that stimulate self-esteem are the same ones that stimulate innovation.

When I sat with a group of managers once, outlining this set of conditions, one of them remarked, "You talk about self-esteem, but what you have described are conditions that stimulate active and creative employee participation—that stimulate innovation."

Precisely. It's all the same issue.

Encouraging the Six Pillars in the Workplace

If managers wish to encourage the practice of the six pillars of self-esteem among those with whom they work, recognizing the benefits to the organization that would result, what actions might they take? The answers that follow are not meant to be exhaustive; they are offered merely as examples of what is possible. Imaginative managers will think of many more items than I have listed here.

To encourage the practice of operating consciously:

- Provide easy access not only to the information people need to do their job, but also about the wider context in which they work—the goals and progress of the organization, market conditions in general, the activities of competitors—so that they are always operating with the clearest grasp of context possible.

- Create an open, interactive environment in which people can share ideas, excitement, and wild fantasies—stimulating everyone's imagination—in contrast to the dominant mood of too many corporations, in which isolation, frustration, and apprehension (fear of not looking good) is the norm.

- Offer opportunities for continual learning and upgrading of skills. Stress the value of study and skill acquisition. Send out the signal in as many ways as possible that yours is a learning organization.

- Allow adequate time for ideas to develop and mature, recognizing that minds have their own timetables.

- If someone does superior work or makes an excellent decision, invite him or her to explore how and why it happened. Do not limit yourself simply to praise. By asking appropriate questions, help raise the person's consciousness about what made the achievement possible, and thereby increase the likelihood that others like it will occur in the future.

- If someone does unacceptable work or makes a bad decision, practice the same principle. Do not limit yourself to corrective feedback. Invite an exploration of what made the error possible, thus raising the level of consciousness and minimizing the likelihood of a repetition.

- Avoid overdirecting, overobserving, and overreporting. Excessive managing *(micromanaging)* is the enemy of autonomy and creativity. You can't push consciousness to the limit with someone else breathing down your neck—and neither can your employees.

- Plan and budget appropriately for innovation. Do not ask for people's innovative best and then announce there is no money or other resources to implement what they come up with—creative enthusiasm (expanded consciousness) will dry up and be replaced by demoralization (shrunken consciousness).

- Stretch your people. Assign tasks and projects slightly beyond their known capabilities. Challenge consciousness to grow. Keep handing responsibility down, projecting confidence in people's ability to think and solve problems on their own.

- Give creative people the opportunity to take as large a part as possible in overall decision-making, thus engaging and utilizing their minds not only with regard to specific problems but also with regard to long-range plans.

To encourage the practice of self-acceptance:

- When you talk with your people, be present to the experience. Make eye contact, listen actively, offer appropriate feedback, give the speaker the experience of being heard and accepted.
- Regardless of who you are talking to, maintain a tone of respect. Do not permit yourself a condescending, superior, sarcastic, or blaming tone.
- Keep encounters regarding work task-centered, not ego-centered. Never permit a dispute to deteriorate into a conflict of personalities. The focus needs to be on reality—What is the situation? What does the work require? What needs to be done?
- Describe undesirable behavior without blaming. Let someone know if his or her behavior is unacceptable: point out its consequences, communicate the kind of behavior you want instead, and omit character assassination.
- Let your people see that you talk honestly about your feelings: if you are hurt or angry or offended, say so straightforwardly and with dignity (and give everyone a lesson in the strength of self-acceptance).

There is power inherent in diversity of approach.

- Recognize and accept differences in individuals. Do not demand that everyone be made from the same mold. Cultivate the ability to identify each person's unique characteristics, and treat each person as having value in his or her own right. Don't let your personality and preferred style of doing things stifle all those who operate differently. Appreciate the power inherent in diversity of approach.

- Develop (in yourself!) greater tolerance for the frustration of mistakes and errors—because without them innovation is impossible. If your people feel mistakes are unacceptable they are very unlikely to achieve anything of importance.

- As much as possible, reward success and ignore failure—except insofar as the latter can be used as a source of learning.

- Invite your people to tell you the kind of manager you are. Model frankness, candor, and nondefensiveness. Find out how you come across and how you could improve—all the while modeling self-acceptance.

- Don't write off or reject the loner. Obviously good team players are necessary and highly useful—but find a place for the creative hermit or chronic outsider. Every organization needs at least a few bright minds that are listening to a different drummer. An accepting attitude toward loners sends a signal to everyone.

To encourage the practice of self-responsibility:

- Communicate that self-responsibility is expected and create opportunities for it. Give your people space to take the initiative, volunteer ideas, and expand their range.

- Set clear and unequivocal performance standards. Let people understand your nonnegotiable expectations regarding the quality of work.

- Elicit from people their understanding of what they are accountable for, so as to assure that their understanding and yours is the same. Elicit a clear statement of what precisely they are committed to being responsible for.

- Encourage people who challenge mainstream assumptions—including the assumptions of higher-ups in your organization. While many companies pay lip service to autonomy and flexibility, their policies often evoke immaturity and dependency. If you genuinely desire creative individuality, reward and promote it.

- Teach perseverance. Encourage people to come back to an unsolved problem again and again. With regard to finding solutions, spread the philosophy of "If not me, who?"

- Allow as much freedom as possible for individuals to guide their own work—and communicate your confidence in their ability to do so appropriately.

- Continuously look for ways to give away power to your people. You can teach self-responsibility without ever mentioning the word.

- Promote on the basis of merit rather than seniority, thus sending out the signal that an individual's future lies to a significant extent in his or her own hands.

- Communicate that you are interested in solutions, not excuses, alibis, or blaming. Publicize and celebrate unusual instances of self-responsibility.[1]

To encourage the practice of self-assertiveness:

- Teach that errors and mistakes are opportunities for learning. What can you learn from what happened? is a question that builds self-esteem, encourages self-assertiveness, expands consciousness, and promotes not repeating mistakes.

- Let your people see that it's safe to make mistakes or say, "I don't know, but I will find out." To evoke fear of error or ignorance is to invite deception, inhibition, and an end to self-assertive creativity.
- Let your people see that it's safe to disagree with you: convey respect for differences of opinion and do not punish dissent.
- Work at changing aspects of the organization's culture that undermine self-assertiveness and self-esteem. Traditional procedures (especially requiring that all significant decisions be passed up the chain of command), originating in an older model of management, may stifle not only self-esteem but also any creativity or innovation, leaving those close to the action disempowered and paralyzed.
- Find out what the central interests of your people are and, whenever possible, match tasks and objectives with individual dispositions. Give people an opportunity to do what they enjoy most and do best; build on people's strengths.

Aim your people—and get out of the way.

- Aim your people—and get out of the way. Let them know you are available if needed but do not impose your presence or involvement gratuitously. Remember that your business is to inspire, coach, and facilitate, not to cater to any impulses you may have always to be center stage. Remember that the measure of your success is their creative self-assertiveness.

- Encourage people to see problems as challenges to their ingenuity. Self-assertiveness entails pushing back on the boundaries that confine us. Creative perseverance is one of the highest forms of self-assertiveness. Treat as a challenge to your own creativeness the task of finding new and powerful ways to get this message across.

To encourage the practice of living purposefully:

- Ask your people what they would need to feel more in control of their work—then, if possible, give it to them. If you want to promote autonomy, excitement, and a strong commitment to goals, empower, empower, empower.

- Give your people the resources, information, and authority to do what you have asked them to do. Remember that there can be no responsibility without power, and nothing can so undermine purposefulness as assigning the first without giving the second.

- Help your people understand how their work relates to the overall mission of the organization, so that they always operate with a grasp of the wider context. In the absence of this grasp of context, it is difficult to sustain purposefulness.

- Encourage everyone to keep measuring results against stated goals and objectives—and disseminate this information widely.

- Remember that innovative behavior can no longer be left to chance. You must explicitly communicate that it is expected. Ask yourself and your people this question: If I were to make innovation my conscious purpose, what would I do (or do differently)?

- Communicate innovative objectives in ways that your people can make real to themselves and enthusiastically sign on for. Again, encourage the question, If I were to make the attainment of these objectives my conscious purpose, what would I need to do? Teach the gospel of converting goals into purposes.

- Find out what an individual's personal purposes at work are (such as the pleasure of meeting difficult challenges, working with stimulating people, having an opportunity to learn and grow) and try to match assignments and projects to those purposes. And communicate explicitly that this is your intention.

- Arrive at an absolutely clear statement of what the problem or goal is, and encourage others to own the problem and to make its innovative solution their personal mission.

To encourage the practice of integrity:

- Exemplify that which you wish to see in others. Tell the truth. Keep promises. Honor commitments. Let there be perceived congruence between what you profess and what you do. And not just with insiders but with everyone you deal with—suppliers, customers, and so on.

- If you make a mistake in your dealings with someone, are unfair or short-tempered, admit it and apologize. Do not imagine (like some autocratic parent) that it would demean your dignity or position to admit taking an action you regret.

- Invite your people to give you feedback on the kind of boss you are. (Remember that you are the kind of manager your people say you are.) Let your people see that you honestly want to know how you affect them, and that you are open to learning and self-correction. Set an example of nondefensiveness. Uphold standards of honesty, integrity, and fair dealing and let it be known that failure to honor these values can be grounds for dismissal, even if one has met one's numbers.

You are the kind of manager your people say you are.

- When mistakes are made, let the appropriate people take responsibility for them. Do not try to cover them up in the name of public image. Remember that everyone can manifest integrity when it's easy; the test comes when it is not easy. That is when you reveal to the world who you are and whether you are really a person who walks his talk. By your own choices and actions, show your people the moral behavior you expect of them. Show the world what kind of organization you have. Everyone understands that individuals and companies make mistakes; the question is what they elect to do about those mistakes: own them and correct them—or try to sweep them under the rug.
- Convey in every way possible that your commitment is to operate as a thoroughly moral company, and look for opportunities to reward and publicize unusual instances of ethical behavior in your people.

Treating Your People as Consultants

One further suggestion that does not fall easily into one or another of the pillars but supports and encourages all of them:

Think of each employee as a consultant—as someone with his or her own perspective on the organization, its practices and its needs, someone who may have something unique to offer, be it a way to cut costs or better serve customers or improve some internal system or adapt existing products to new uses, to fill some unnoticed niche in the marketplace or modify the workspace in such a way as to facilitate and stimulate greater creative interaction among people.

Think of the impact on self-esteem and on the motivation to contribute of being treated in this manner.

One Last Suggestion: Focus on Strengths

Among Peter Drucker's encyclopedic contributions to the field of management—indeed Drucker is credited with being the creator of management as a discipline—one of his most important ideas is that managers should focus on people's strengths instead of their weaknesses. Rather than dwell on the areas where a worker is weak, says Drucker, find out what he does well, determine the context in which he is able to exercise his positive capabilities—and let him do it. Make his shortcomings irrelevant. The function of an organization is to make human strength productive—and this is accomplished by building on people's assets, not by bemoaning their limitations.

Focus on people's strengths instead of their weaknesses.

This idea is a superb illustration of the principle that the practices that serve high performance are also the practices that serve self-esteem—and vice versa. Effective psychotherapists know that they help clients grow in self-esteem by identifying and releasing resources—positive potentials. Effective managers know that they inspire the best performance when they release people to do what they do well. And if healthy self-esteem supports high performance, pride in one's competence—and in a job well done—supports self-esteem.

As an aside about Peter Drucker, when I first read his great classics *The Practice of Management* and *Innovation and Entrepreneurship* and was struck by the persuasiveness of his ideas, the thought that kept recurring was: Who are the giants who will put into practice what he is advocating? It seemed obvious to me that a substantial level of self-esteem would be required not merely to agree with his proposals but to act on them. Very little in our educational system or in most people's upbringing prepares them for operating at Drucker's level in the workplace. This realization greatly strengthened my conviction concerning the new importance of self-esteem in an information economy.

Why Managers Fail

It is one thing to understand the ideas offered here and another to put them into practice. A major step in operating consciously and self-responsibly is the willingness to examine yourself and identify what might be the internal obstacles needing to be overcome. Your deepest vision of yourself—of what is possible and appropriate to you—again we are talking about self-esteem—will most certainly need to be considered.

There are many reasons managers may not do their job well. One reason is that they have never been properly trained. Another is that they do not really like managing *people*, they like managing technology or finance or logistics or anything but human beings. Another is that they lack emotional intelligence—that is, lack emotional self-awareness, do not know how to manage their own feelings, are not sensitive to others' emotions and needs. While not all managerial problems are traceable to self-esteem problems, it is impressive how often they are, in whole or in part.

Some years ago a study was done of 191 top executives in Fortune 500 companies who had suffered some career setback, from missed promotions to business failures.[2] The study identified five fundamental causes. Significantly, none had to do with the technical side of the work; as a group the managers in the study were as technically competent as those who succeeded. The causes all had to do with the human or psychological aspect of their job. Although the report did not say so, all five causes had self-esteem implications worth pondering. Some of these points were anticipated earlier in our discussion but they bear repeating.

1. *The biggest single cause of failure was poor interpersonal skills:* inability to inspire; poor listening; doesn't give or receive criticism well; fearful of conflict, therefore avoids confrontation and the raising of important issues likely to produce agitation.

This describes a person who does not bring respect or benevolence to human encounters; who operates out of fear and insecurity, not out of confidence and respect for facts; and who lacks the level of self-awareness that is a prerequisite of dealing effectively with others. With such liabilities, an executive cannot create the climate of respect that is the foundation of high performance among knowledge workers.

2. *An inability to change, to let go of strategies that are no longer adaptive:* failure to respond appropriately to the new and unfamiliar (like the GE executives described earlier).

Rigidity is a characteristic of a mind that lacks confidence in itself and therefore lacks confidence in its ability to cope with new and unfamiliar challenges. Poor self-esteem clings to the security of the known; high self-esteem sees change as an opportunity and even an adventure. We cannot lead others where we are afraid to go ourselves. An executive who dreads change is not a force for progress in an organization but a force for demoralization and apathy. Instead of inspiring confidence, a fearful executive inspires fear and inertia.

We cannot lead others where we are afraid to go ourselves.

3. *A preoccupation with self-aggrandizement or turf-protection at the expense of the needs of the organization.*

However rationalized, this represents a betrayal of trust and a failure of integrity. It also implies a belief that one is not good enough to succeed on objective performance alone. Often this behavior is associated with an overreliance on external validation—one's position is valued above everything. It would be an error to assume that a person preoccupied with protecting turf has an excess of self-esteem. Nonstop self-absorption, narcissism, or grandiosity—all signifying absence of objectivity—are not expressions of self-esteem but evidence of its lack.

4. *A fear of making decisions and taking action—one of the commonest causes of business failure.*

What is this fear but lack of confidence in one's mind and judgment?

5. *Lack of resilience and the ability to rebound from adversity and setbacks.*

Disappointments in business (as in life) are inevitable. The level of our self-esteem has a great deal to do with how we are likely to react to them. The executives who failed to get promoted or who lost their jobs were the ones who in the face of problems did not search for solutions but instead fell into defensiveness, alibiing, and blaming others, or else into depression and passivity. This is typical behavior of people who lack trust in their own resourcefulness.

Whether the issue of self-esteem is identified explicitly or not, and usually it is not, its importance in the workplace can hardly be overstated.

Ideas for Managers

When I am asked by companies to teach how self-esteem principles and technology can be used to stimulate better performance, I often ask participants—by way of an introductory demonstration—to write six to ten endings for sentence stems such as the following:

If I bring 5 percent more consciousness to my dealings with people today—

If I operate with 5 percent greater self-acceptance today—

If I operate 5 percent more self-responsibly with people today—

If I operate 5 percent more self-assertively with people today—

If I operate 5 percent more purposefully with people today—

If I bring 5 percent more integrity to my dealings with people today—

Stems such as these and dozens of others like them invariably stimulate a direct experience of what the practice of the six pillars means, not only for self-esteem, but also for productivity and interpersonal effectiveness. They are useful for managers who wish to work on themselves, and also as an exercise for those who report to them; in other words, they are useful for anyone on any level.

For the stem *If I bring 5 percent more consciousness to my dealings with people today—* it is very common to get endings such as:

—I would listen more.

—I would be more sensitive.

—I would notice how I affect people.

—I would be a better communicator.

—I think I would be more relaxed, less impatient, and more benevolent.

—I would notice what works and what doesn't work when dealing with people.

For the stem *If I operate with 5 percent greater self-acceptance today*— typical endings include:

—I'd be more accepting of others.

—I wouldn't generate so much heat.

—I'd be calmer.

—not everything would be such a big deal.

—I'd be kinder.

—encounters would be more human.

—I'd be more open to hearing.

—I think I'd be less on the defensive.

—I could handle critical feedback better.

For the stem *If I operate 5 percent more self-responsibly with people today*— typical endings include:

—I'd take pains to be sure I was understood and not blame others when I wasn't.

—I'd look at what I'm avoiding.

—I'd get more done.

—I'd control my priorities and not let people throw me off for no good reason.

—I'd give up blaming and examine myself more.

—I wouldn't permit myself alibis.

—I'd carry my own weight and require that others carry theirs.

—I'd stay focused on results.

—I'd be a better team player.

—I'd not expect people to be mind-readers, I'd let them know what I was thinking or expecting or needing.

—I'd pay more attention to the quality of my communications.

For the stem *If I operate 5 percent more self-assertively with people today*— typical endings include:

—I'd be more candid.

—I wouldn't drag my feet about declaring bad news.

—if I didn't understand, I'd ask questions rather than pretend I knew.

—when I knew something impossible was being asked of me, I'd say so on the spot.

—I'd be more honest about my feelings.

—if someone wasn't doing the job that was needed, I'd be faster to react and insist on better performance.

—I'd be clear about my expectations and I'd lay them right out there.

—when I knew I had done a good job, I'd make sure my bosses knew about it.

—if I know I need something from the company to do the best job possible, I'd say so, I'd ask for it.

—I wouldn't be wishy-washy about presenting my ideas at meetings, I'd stand up for them.

For the stem *If I operate 5 percent more purposefully with people today*— typical endings include:

—I'd want to know the purpose of any meeting or conversation and I'd try to keep us on track.

—my work would be more focused on results.

—I'd prioritize my time better.

—I'd tell people when they wandered away from the subject.

—I'd encourage my people to stay conscious of their goals and not get distracted.

—I'd stay focused on my job and not get bogged down doing other people's work.

—I'd look at everything from the perspective of how it affects long-term goals.

For the stem *If I bring 5 percent more integrity to my dealings with people today*— typical endings include:

—I'd be more careful about the promises I make or the assurances I give.

—I wouldn't BS when talking to customers.

—I'd think more about what's fair and not act so much on impulse.

—I'd stand up for my people.

—people would know my word was my bond.

—I'd be a person I could admire more.

—I wouldn't alibi.

—I'd act on what I know.

—people would have more confidence in me and more trust.

—I wouldn't go unconscious to escape unpleasantness.

After people have written endings for all of these stems and get an idea of how sentence completion works, I typically suggest that they work on one stem for a week, writing six to ten endings Monday through Friday, then move on to the next stem the following week, and so on. That repetition is essential for going deeper into the material, facilitating lasting integration, and stimulating changes of behavior. It is often helpful to have people meet for an hour at the end of the week in groups of two or three to share and discuss their endings, because this drives the work still further toward desired results.

When consultants or managers elect to experiment with exercises such as these, they are often astonished at how much people know that they do not know they know, how much insight and wisdom seems to lie just below the surface of awareness. The challenge is not so much to teach new management skills that no one has heard of before as it is to liberate what people already know and remove the barriers to their acting on it.

When sentence-completion responses are shared in a group and

People know a great deal that they do not know they know.

the group embarks on a brainstorming session aimed at answering questions like How do we translate these learnings into action? How do we overcome fears? and How do we keep ourselves on track? a team leader discovers how much creative intelligence often lies unused because it was not expected by anyone or because no one believed it was there.

When we project the conviction that people are capable of far more than they give themselves credit for, we facilitate their activating resources of which they were unaware—with the result of improved performance and improved self-esteem.

Take the problem of turf-protection mentioned earlier. I was once asked to work with three gifted senior managers who were inclined to protect their own territory, sometimes at the expense of the best interests of the company. Although the matter had been discussed with them, nothing changed. I had them participate in a day-long seminar during which, among other things, they did an exercise in which they were asked to imagine that they each had a manager with this problem; they were to devise strategies they thought could inspire the change they desired. This included thinking through every type of resistance they were likely to encounter and how they would deal with it. Then they were asked to write a report on what they had learned from the experience. This was followed by private, one-on-one debriefings, in which the experience and the learnings were reviewed. The three manifested a higher level of insight than they had ever displayed before. They themselves located where the leverage was to induce a change in their behavior. Their resistance, while it did not disappear entirely, was significantly diminished because they did not experience the pressure to change as coming exclusively from the outside; they felt it within themselves—which was the ultimate intention of the exercise.

One of the ways we encourage self-responsibility, stimulate creativity, and facilitate constructive change is to find ways to give a problem back to the person who created it—as we saw, for instance, in the story of the eight managers I told earlier, and as we can see again in the turf-protection example.

On a very basic level, how we communicate can significantly affect the measure of self-responsibility we draw out of the person with whom we are interacting. The head of the collections department in a company where I consulted presented the following problem to her manager. While she was well liked by everyone and no one wanted to see her fired, she was aversive to simple confrontation, slow to insist on better cooperation from recalcitrant bill-payers, and slow to report her growing list of problem accounts to her boss. I sat in a meeting where she was encouraged, scolded, implored, lectured to, hugged, and rebuked—all to no avail. She just sat there, looking forlorn and helpless. I was asked to intervene. Here is the essence of the conversation that followed:

NB: Alice, do you understand the problem we're faced with? *[My manner is warm and friendly, as it remains throughout; my purpose here is to get Alice and me in the same context.]*

ALICE: Yes, I'm just too shy and I find it hard to . . . you know, get tough. . . . I'm just not the kind of person who— *[Breaks off; silence]*

NB: No, that's not the problem. *[I perceive Alice as wanting to switch the focus to her insecurities and I believe it would be counterproductive for me to follow her down that road.]*

ALICE: It isn't?

NB: The problem is, your job has certain requirements that are not being met. Your job entails having delinquent payers appropriately dealt with. It requires reports on all accounts, especially where there are difficulties. And letting your manager know when there's a problem you need help with. *[I am keeping the focus on the reality we need to deal with.]*

ALICE: Yes, uh-huh.

NB: And right now that's not happening. The job that's needed is not being done. *[No personal reproaches; just a description of the facts.]*

ALICE: Yes, I suppose that's so.

NB: Now it's possible that an error has been made, not by you but by the people who put you in your present position. It just may not be the right job for you. *[I am laying the foundation for giving responsibility to Alice concerning what is ultimately to happen: it will be up to her to tell us whether she is the right person for the job.]*

ALICE: But I love my job.

NB: Yes and no one here wants to lose you. You understand that? Everyone will feel badly if it should prove necessary to replace you. But the job has got to be done right. Nothing to negotiate about there. Because what is being asked for is both necessary and reasonable. And that means the job has to be done by a person who can do it. The only question is: Are you that person? And the only person who can answer is you. *[Firm, friendly, holding Alice to the point at issue; staying focused on the one and only question: can she and will she do the job that needs to be done?]*

ALICE: I can do the job.

NB: Why do you say that? In important ways, you haven't done it so far. *[Challenging her to justify herself, but speaking gently and matter-of-factly.]*

ALICE: I can do the job. I want the job.

NB: We understand that you want the job and that's good to hear. *[We want someone who strongly wants the job, as Alice does.]* You want the job and you want to do it right. *[In the second half of the statement I am imputing to her the conscientiousness that is needed, hoping she will rise to the occasion, as she does.]*

ALICE: Yes.

NB: And yet, it's been difficult for you to do the job. Don't you think it will be just as difficult tomorrow and next week? *[I continue to test the strength of her motivation.]*

ALICE: No. Because I see that it's really necessary and, you know, if I really make up my mind to do something, I can do it. The problem in the past was, I made up my mind I couldn't do it. Now I'm going to make up my mind I can do it. And I know I can.

NB: What do you think would be an appropriate response if you don't do it? *[Asking her to look at the situation from the perspective of the needs of the organization.]*

ALICE: The job will have to be given to someone else. It's got to be done right. I see that. And I'm going to do it right.

NB: Great. We'll all be pulling for you. Shall we agree that you'll review your progress with your manager two weeks from this coming Friday? *[Encouraging her while keeping us focused on the matter of accountability.]*

ALICE: I really see it's nothing personal.

NB: Thank you for understanding that. *[Acknowledging and appreciating her, but as an adult speaking to an adult.]*

The best way to evoke rationality is to project the expectation that it is going to be forthcoming.

It would not have been helpful to become embroiled in discussions of Alice's psychology. Also, to do so could have been intrusive and invasive and therefore immoral (however kind the intention). The focus had to be on objective reality: the requirements of the job—and Alice's performance. This helped Alice to stay focused on the fact that if she couldn't do what was needed, someone else would have to replace her, no matter how well liked she was—because the work had to be done. And Alice's stronger self came through, which is what often happens when you talk to the rational adult in a person. The best way to evoke rationality is to project the expectation that it is going to be forthcoming. When we project the opposite, we often produce a self-fulfilling prophecy. After the meeting, in private, I asked Alice if in any way she felt I was tough on her. She answered, "No. I felt you respected me enough to talk straight."

• • • • • • •

In this chapter and the preceding one I give examples of some of the ways sentence-completion work can be used to facilitate self-understanding and behavior change. At the end of the book, you will find a full-length sentence-completion program for personal and professional self-development. Among its other purposes, this program will help in integrating many of the ideas presented here.

But first, in Chapter Five, I want to discuss certain themes I have touched on briefly and now want to elaborate on: managing change, creating a culture of accountability, supporting innovation, and treating work as a vehicle for growth and self-actualization.

5

Rising to Challenges

There should be nothing surprising in my choice of the four topics mentioned at the end of the preceding chapter: managing change, creating a culture of accountability, supporting innovation, and treating work as a vehicle for growth and self-actualization. Change is the ultimate challenge facing business organizations today. And change and its vicissitudes cannot be mastered without a culture of accountability and innovation. And these realities generate the need for higher levels of psychological development than were ever needed before—so that working on oneself and working at one's job are not unrelated.

I will begin with a few general observations:

If we cannot manage ourselves, we are unfit to manage others.

If we are blind to our own feelings and emotions, we will be blind to the feelings and emotions of others.

If we do not have the discipline to keep ourselves task-focused, we will not be able to inspire that focus in others.

If we cannot keep our own spirits up in the face of adversity, we cannot sustain hope and courage in those who look to us for leadership.

If we are cynical about ourselves, we will be cynical about others—and inspire cynicism in them.

If we do not model self-responsibility, we cannot teach it.

If we do not exemplify integrity, we cannot inspire it in others.

Therefore, what an honest manager (or leader) must ask is: Do my actions embody the principles that I wish to see exemplified in those I manage?

If you accept these observations, you see some of the moral and psychological challenges that confront you in the workplace—for example, the need for responsibility and accountability, the importance of integrity and trust, the imperative of innovation—as well as some of the opportunities for growth and development.

Change is the ultimate challenge facing business organizations today.

Change

I have already observed that any significant change constitutes a challenge to our confidence in our resourcefulness. One aspect of what I refer to is the fact that for millions of people this is a time of disorienting transition: old jobs disappear, familiar skills became obsolete, new opportunities appear demanding new knowledge and new talents—sometimes at a dizzying rate. This is one of the many reasons self-esteem has become so important today.

The most significant change that has taken place in the past few decades is not any particular political, technological, or economic development, dramatic though such developments have been. The most important change is in the rate of change itself, the fact that change keeps happening faster and faster and that turbulence—not to say chaos—must now be recognized and adapted to as the norm.

It is one thing to adapt to any particular change that is perceived to be necessary; it is another—and more demanding—to adapt to a major escalation in the rate of change itself even when it is perceived to be inescapable. Yet that is what is now required.

The first step in responding appropriately is to recognize that resistance to change is not intrinsically pathological. Often it is entirely normal. Think of the role of homeostasis in the human body: its function is to protect the organism against the storms of change that would disrupt normal functioning and the structural integrity of the whole. The simplest illustration of what I mean is our temperature, which fluctuates within extremely narrow limits. If body temperature drops below normal, homeostatic processes immediately swing into action aimed at causing it to rise; if body temperature rises above normal, homeostatic processes go into action aimed at bringing it down. In this sense, biological functions are essentially conservative: they aim at preserving what exists.

The most important change is in the rate of change itself.

A similar process is at work when an individual clings to familiar survival strategies that have in some sense worked in the past—for example, inappropriate obedience to authority figures—in the face of evidence that those strategies are now obsolete and may even be harmful. We do not readily give up that which we see as having protected us and facilitated our well-being. So we may repeat behaviors that make no sense in terms of our present context, while rejecting proposed alternatives that better serve our interests but that are new and unfamiliar, such as learning to think for ourselves and be more self-assertive.

Similarly, families, organizations, and societies evolve or establish patterns that, once in place, do not readily yield to novelty. The status quo does not abdicate merely because change comes knocking at the door, announcing the need for new courses of action.

And, as I have already suggested, there is a healthy element in this conservatism; it protects that which exists; it guards against instability; it never embraces change for the sake of change.

But of course in individuals and in social groups there are changes that are desirable and indisputably necessary. And often the resistance with which they are met represents more than healthy homeostasis: the anxiety of underdeveloped self-esteem and fear of the new and unfamiliar.

When effective psychotherapists encounter this fear in their clients they treat it with respect: they understand that the organism is merely striving—even if in a misguided way—to take care of itself. We have learned that a resistance that is respected is far easier to dissolve than one we simply try to bull our way through. Once an individual sees that his or her fear (resistance) is not ridiculed or dismissed but is treated with empathy, the mind relaxes and opens to considering alternative ways of responding. A resistance that is condemned grows stronger; one that is accepted begins to weaken.

I am thinking of a gifted engineer I had occasion to work with not long ago. Growing up in an irrational and chaotic home environment—what we typically call a dysfunctional family—he learned a particular survival strategy that seemed to protect him. In effect, he created a private world for himself in which people counted for very little and the ability to understand and manipulate physical reality was a source of security, satisfaction, and self-esteem. Because his work was so brilliant his company promoted him from engineer to manager of engineers. This immediately plunged him into anxiety and depression. The managerial training his company had provided, which might have been adequate under different circumstances, failed completely in this case because his self-concept could not accommodate his achieving interpersonal competence. That's not who I am, he told himself. He saw himself as a man who did not relate well to others—period. At the same time, he valued the advantages that went with his new position and said he wanted to master the skills his position required. That was the conflict that led him to my office. To assist him in expanding his vision of what was possible to him, I first had to enter into his perspective, into his experience of reality, not to fight his overlimited self-concept but to relate to it empathetically. Only when he felt understood and accepted on his own terms did his mind relax and open to considering other possibilities. He became free to see his private world mentality as a strategy that had served him once but had become obsolete. This was the first essential step on the road to the change his rational self desired.

If you are an executive who carries the responsibility for leading necessary change in your organization, the place to begin is with self-examination, with the question: Are there parts of me that resist and are in rebellion against this change, even though my mind sees that the change is necessary? You might even experiment with sentence completion: *One of the bad things about making this change (or these changes) is—* Give your reservations a hearing; give them their day in court; articulate them and meditate on them, without self-reproach.

Another mind-clearing sentence stem I have found useful is: *One of the ways I could undermine the changes I am advocating is—*

In raising the level of your self-awareness, you will increase the likelihood of successfully implementing the changes you are committed to. And you will not be simultaneously engaged in self-sabotage. You will neither be sending contradictory messages to your people nor engaging in contradictory behavior. The discipline of taking yourself through this process raises the level of your consciousness, strengthens your self-esteem, and helps clear the way for you to perform effectively.

When working with others in an organization to accept and implement necessary changes, it is imperative that the reasons for the changes—their necessity—be made abundantly clear. This may need to be explained not once but many times. Questions will need to be treated respectfully—and answered patiently. Since what you require is not obedience but cooperation, it must always be held in the foreground of your awareness that you are addressing minds.

What change requires is not obedience but cooperation.

In small or large group discussions, people should be invited to examine and articulate their misgivings. If there are fears, they should be honored rather than ridiculed or dismissed peremptorily. Sometimes it is useful to design exercises that allow people to struggle with the new circumstances that create the need for changes in the organization—for example, lay out all the relevant facts and invite them to define options, project consequences, and produce solutions—so that they are led to see for themselves what needs to be done and thereby lose the sense of having something imposed on them from above.

That the changes represent a challenge to their self-esteem should be named explicitly. People should be helped to understand how their sense of their own resourcefulness—the level of their confidence in their minds—affects their responses.

Just as the new challenges confronting the organization can be framed not as tragedies but as opportunities (which is how change-masters see things), the new responses required of individuals can be understood not as burdens or problems but as vehicles for personal growth. This is the perspective that yields the experience of personal power in times of turbulence.

Accountability

If the need to master change is one of the great challenges of the twenty-first-century organization, another is to create a culture of self-responsibility and personal accountability.

When people operate self-responsibly and accountably, it is a win both for them personally and for the organization that employs them. I have already suggested some of the ways self-responsibility can be encouraged. Here I want to amplify a bit how one goes about creating a culture of self-responsibility and accountability.

Leaders and managers must exemplify that which they wish to create around them.

First and foremost—this point can never be overstressed—leaders and managers must exemplify that which they wish to create around them, that which they wish to see in others. This means:

- Being proactive rather than reactive
- Manifesting a high level of consciousness, focus, and purpose
- Taking responsibility for every choice, decision, and action without blaming or finding alibis
- Being fully accountable for all promises and commitments made
- Being clear on what is and is not within their power
- Being task-focused rather than focused on self-aggrandizement
- Being results-focused rather than turf-protecting
- Being able to bounce back from defeat, setbacks, or adversity and continue moving toward goals, rather than surrendering to despair
- Demonstrating an unmistakable commitment to facing reality, whether pleasant or unpleasant

When these traits are present in leaders and managers, the result is much the same as when they are modeled by parents in a family: a context is established in which it is most likely that these traits will be absorbed and exhibited by others. The conclusion is drawn: This is how human beings are to act; this is the norm here; this is what is expected of me.

But there is more to the process of creating an organizational culture of accountability than appropriate modeling. Leaders and managers have to think through the policies that will inspire the desired mind-set among employees. Here are just a few basics (with apologies for the repetitions and overlapping I have found inescapable):

- *Require clarity concerning what is expected.* This means that leaders and managers must be absolutely clear, and see to it that the relevant persons are absolutely clear, about what each individual in an organization is accountable for.

Some years ago the CEO of a medium-sized business gave me the assignment of finding out why there was not a higher level of accountability in his firm and what could be done about it. I suggested that we begin by asking each of his senior managers to write a memo stating what precisely they understood themselves to be responsible for and also what they would like to be responsible for. What surfaced immediately was tremendous confusion. In some instances, two or more executives held themselves exclusively responsible for the same aspect of the business; but for other aspects, no one claimed responsibility. In other words, some areas were given too much attention, which led to one kind of problem, while other areas were neglected, which led to another kind of problem. The next step was to review, redefine, and gain agreement concerning each person's area of accountability. This process was repeated with all the people who reported to each of these managers. The same kind of memo was requested, the same kind of confusion was uncovered, and the same remedial action was taken. Until each person knew what was expected of him or her, there could be no question of appropriate accountability.

• *Seek information regarding people's work goals*. When you ask people what they would like to be accountable for, you can sometimes elicit useful information about their aspirations and ambitions. The best people in any organization are always looking to move beyond their job descriptions and, whenever possible, this is an attitude to be nurtured and supported. Give people all the responsibilities they can reasonably handle. Ask more of them and support them in asking more of themselves.

• *Be task-centered, not ego-centered*. When we keep our encounters focused on reality and the objective needs of the situation, we support a climate of self-responsibility rather than permitting a dispute to deteriorate into a conflict of personalities. The focus should be on What are the facts? What needs to be done? and not Whose wishes will prevail—yours or mine? The individual should ask, "What are my reasons for taking this position?" and not, "What is my rank in the organization?"

• *Invite feedback on the kind of boss, leader, and manager you are*. Let your people see that you are honestly interested in the image you project and how you affect others. Let them know you understand the principle that "you are the kind of manager your people say you are." Let them know that if they have a grievance against you, you expect them to communicate it as quickly as possible—and set an example of open, nondefensive listening. Convey that you have little tolerance for grievances that are never expressed but that fester privately into bitterness and resentment. Exemplify self-responsibility in this area and make it clear that you require it of others.

• *Give corrective feedback without blaming*. If someone's behavior is unacceptable, describe it, point out its consequences, including how other people are affected, and spell out the kind of behavior you require instead. Stay focused on fact and avoid character assassination.

Communicate the belief that your listener would want to know if his or her behavior is undesirable, troublesome, or offensive. By keeping the focus on reality and avoiding put-downs or personal attacks, you speak to the self-responsible adult in the other party and discourage an evasive or defensive response.

- *Help people experience themselves as the source of their actions and tune them in to the why*. If someone does superior work or makes an excellent decision, do not limit yourself to praise, but invite him or her to explore how and why it happened. Ask appropriate questions to help the person identify what made the achievement possible. For example, what was the mental process behind it? As a result, the person doesn't write off the achievement to luck but experiences himself or herself as the responsible causal agent, and you thereby increase the likelihood that the behavior will be repeated. By the same logic, if someone does unacceptable work or makes a bad decision, practice the same principle. Do not limit yourself to corrective feedback—invite an exploration of what caused the error, again stressing responsibility, in this case minimizing the chance of a repetition.
- *Establish clear and unequivocal performance standards*. This is one aspect of the wider use of communicating people's responsibilities. Employees need to know a leader's (or manager's or boss's) nonnegotiable expectations regarding the quality of work. They need to know that this is the minimum expected of them. Nonaccountability at this level is completely unacceptable.
- *Let problems stay with the person who created them*. When someone's behavior creates a problem, ask him or her to provide a solution, if possible. Try to avoid handing down ready-made solutions that spare the person from taking a new initiative or developing new ideas. Instead, say, "Now that we agree on the nature of the problem, what do you propose to do about it?" Do not deny people the experience of learning from their struggle with this question.

- *Focus on finding solutions, not blaming.* When things go wrong, the question should not be, Whose fault is it? but What needs to be done? Convey in every way possible that blaming is an irrelevant distraction. The name of the game is results, not accusations. Ask, "What are your ideas on how this situation can be improved or corrected?"
- *Give people the resources for self-responsibility.* People cannot be accountable for what you have asked them to do if they are not given the appropriate resources, information, and authority. Remember that there is no responsibility without power. It is demoralizing to give people the first but not the second. An occasional hero will rise above circumstances and assert a power that no one has given him or her, taking responsibility and exercising ingenuity and initiative far beyond the call of duty. But it is unfair and

There is no responsibility without power.

unreasonable of management to count on that.
- *Remember what your job is.* A great leader is not someone who comes up with brilliant solutions but rather one who inspires his or her people to come up with brilliant solutions. Like a great coach, a great parent, or a great psychotherapist, a great leader draws out the best in people but does not do their work for them. Sometimes, if you are the leader or manager, this means controlling your exhibitionistic impulses or desire to be admired.
- *Work at changing aspects of the organizational culture that thwart or frustrate self-responsibility.* Sometimes outmoded procedures carried over from the command-and-control management model frustrate the self-responsibility that you are promoting. When significant decision-making must be passed up the chain of command, those close to the decision are disempowered and paralyzed.

Such policies stifle innovation and creativity, and make personal accountability all but impossible.

- *Avoid micromanagement.* Micromanagement is the enemy of autonomy and self-responsibility. If you want people to operate self-responsibly, avoid overdirecting, overobserving, overreporting, and overmanaging. Let people know what needs to be done and leave them alone. Let people struggle. Let them take the initiative in asking for help if and when they need it, but do not take the decision out of their hands. Just as parents who overmanage a young person can obstruct evolution to adulthood, so leaders who micromanage inhibit the very traits they need most for the success of the enterprise. Young people learn self-responsibility in part by being trusted; so do men and women in an organization. When a leader conveys belief in people's competence and worth, people are far more likely to rise to the occasion. Do not step in unless it is absolutely necessary.
- *Plan and budget for innovation.* It is unreasonable to ask for self-responsibility, initiative, innovation, and creativity and then announce that there are no resources to support and implement the contributions people make. The predictable result is that people will fall into (relative) passivity and demoralization. Organizations need to make self-responsibility practical.
- *Find out what people want and need to perform optimally, and provide it.* The less people feel in control of their work, the more they grow dispirited, unambitious, unempowered, and unable to self-generate. One of the most useful questions to ask people is, "What do you need to feel more in control of your work?" If possible, give it to them. If what you want from people is excitement, autonomy, and a personal stake in the success of your company, try to give them what they need to achieve these things.
- *Reward self-responsible behavior.* Reward self-assertiveness, intelligent risk-taking, acts of initiative, unsolicited problem solving, and a strong orientation toward action. Too many companies pay lip service to these values but in practice reward those who conform, don't ask difficult questions, don't challenge the status quo,

and remain essentially passive while going through the motions of their job description. If you want to create a culture of innovation and responsibility, look for opportunities to reward and celebrate it. Let your responses signal *That is what we want*. When people do things right in important or original ways, broadcast their stories through your entire organization. No aspect of an organization's culture is more revealing than the kind of stories that circulate.

No aspect of an organization's culture reveals more than the kind of stories that circulate.

By now it will be obvious that every one of these suggestions, aimed at supporting self-responsibility and personal accountability, also supports self-esteem—supports an individual's experience of competence and worth. Organizations that support self-esteem attract the best people and tend to keep them. There is no mystery as to why. Not if you understand the importance of self-esteem to the feeling of personal fulfillment.

Creativity and Innovation

As with the issues of managing change and creating a culture of accountability, I have already made a number of suggestions about how creativity and innovation can be nurtured in an organization. What follows are only a few concluding observations.

Successful business organizations know that to remain competitive in world markets they need a steady stream of innovation in products, services, and internal systems. It is now recognized that these must be planned for as a normal part of business operations. Here, let us consider some personal aspects of creativity and innovation.

What do we know about the characteristics of the creative and innovative mind?

Research informs us, and it is hardly surprising, that one of the traits of creative, innovative persons is intelligence significantly above the average. One of the most frequently cited sources of work satisfaction among such individuals is the opportunity to interact with other high-level knowledge workers who provide challenge and stimulation—as well as the opportunity to pit their minds and energies against those of their counterparts working for competitors.

They tend to possess a high level of imaginativeness, which plays an important role in creative thinking. So time and opportunities to engage in mental play can be important to generating results.

They tend to think outside the box, to ignore conventional or standard "sets," and to look at things in new and unexpected ways—which means that an overly conformist business culture is deadly to the innovator. Management must learn how to accommodate independent minds—by creating an environment in which such minds can feel comfortable, valued, and appreciated, without ignoring or violating the basic structures and procedures that an organization legitimately requires.

An overly conformist business culture is deadly to the innovator.

Creative and innovative people tend to notice problems that others have failed to notice and to ask questions others failed to raise—and thereby to provoke envy, jealousy, or irritation, which others must learn to self-manage. Which leads to another challenge for management: keeping everyone mission-focused, task-focused, and integrity-focused, so that personal feelings of resentment are not allowed to sabotage the larger goals. This is accomplished, first and foremost, by the values management upholds and exemplifies.

Creative and innovative people also tend to manifest significant autonomy and independence. Important management implication: creativity does not like to take orders.

They tend to have highly integrative minds and to see connections between seemingly unrelated elements. One is reminded of Aristotle's observation concerning the relationship between genius and the ability to think metaphorically. Management implication: don't be in a hurry to dismiss ideas that at first seem strange.

Creative and innovative people tend to be persevering and to be stimulated by the challenges of hard work. So one of the ways to inspire their best is to offer projects that push them to the outer limits of their known abilities—and beyond.

They have made themselves highly knowledgeable in the field where their creativity and innovativeness finds expression. The only qualification one might want to enter here is that sometimes ignorance can work to one's advantage; not knowing that experts have found something to be unachievable, young people may blithely proceed to achieve it—which is one reason for hiring lots of young people and throwing apparently impossible problems at them; but still, young people do require knowledge and expertise in their own domain.

Creative and innovative people operate far more by intrinsic than by extrinsic motivation in the process of creativity and innovation; growth and achievement needs matter more than praise or monetary rewards, without denying the latter may be important. Which means: give them freedom, give them resources, give them a stimulating environment—and give them an exciting and inspiring mountain to climb.

A number of the traits described in this section clearly relate to self-esteem, such as autonomy and intrinsic motivation. And just as it is not surprising that the kind of individual I am describing tends to have superior intelligence, so it is not surprising that he or she tends to manifest a decent level of self-esteem, although not necessarily or invariably. Creative work is sometimes not so much an expression of self-esteem as an unconscious effort to heal psychic wounds originating early in life; still, some significant measure of self-esteem has to be present for this particular self-healing strategy to be sought: it is not a path likely to be sought by a mind that has no trust in itself.

No single trait mentioned here is always present, but it is doubtful if you will find a highly creative and innovative person in whom most are not present.

It is the task of management to create a context in which creativity and innovation can flourish. Virtually every suggestion offered in this book relates, directly or indirectly, to that goal. The context entails everything from a philosophy that encourages creative activity to the specific policies, systems, procedures, and resources without which creative activity cannot take place. Since the organization necessarily has its own mission and goals, a delicate balance must be maintained between creative freedom on one hand, and, on the other, the restraints required by the organization's overall agenda. There are any number of ways this balance can be addressed and there is no single formula for all situations. What is imperative, however, is that the need for a balance be recognized and that a leader be able to answer how it is achieved in his or her company. The challenge of finding this balance itself represents an opportunity for creativity and innovation.

Work as a Vehicle for Personal Development

There is no serious endeavor, from work to marriage to child-rearing, that cannot be approached as a vehicle for personal growth—just as there is no serious endeavor to which the six pillars of self-esteem are not applicable. There is, for example, no aspect of life that does not confront us with the choice to think or not to think, to raise consciousness or to lower it, to open to reality or to close against it.

Thus, if you were to choose your work as the arena in which you will cultivate the six pillars—meaning integrate them into your daily practice—then your work would benefit while you as a human benefited. You would grow professionally at the same time that you grow personally. Achievement would rise and self-esteem would rise. In this sense, work has the potential of being a spiritual discipline—if that is how it is approached.

By way of illustration, consider the endings you might write for the stems:

If I were to bring 5 percent more integrity to my daily activities—

If I were to bring 5 percent more integrity to my dealings with people—

If I were to bring 5 percent more integrity to my communications—

If I act without integrity—

If I wish to be perceived as honest and trustworthy—

If a concern to grow in integrity is not a concern of the spirit, I do not know what is. It is also a concern with profound ramifications for business success.

Soul-work is essential to meeting the challenges of an information economy.

When I first gave seminars for organizations on the ideas in this book, where the assignment given to me was to focus primarily on business implications and applications, I noticed that on the feedback sheets there was often a line to the effect of "I wish he had talked more about how one builds self-esteem in oneself." There was evidently a hunger for the personal aspects of self-esteem work that I needed to address more. And so in this book I have striven to collapse the distinction between the professional and the personal by stressing that when you overcome fear or inertia to master new ways of operating at work you are strengthening self-esteem. And when you commit yourself to practicing the six pillars in any aspect of your existence you are growing as a person in ways that will have positive results at work, because you will approach work with a higher level of self-esteem. The conclusion I want you to draw from this book is that soul-work is essential to meeting the challenges of an information economy.

In a world in which change is happening all around us, and faster and faster, our openness to change within ourselves, to letting go of irrelevant attachments, to learning and growing as a way of life becomes a personal and professional imperative.

With so many business books quoting famed chairman and CEO of General Electric Jack Welch these days, I am reluctant to summon his voice once more—but somewhere he made an observation too perfect not to cite in concluding this discussion:

"When the rate of change outside exceeds the rate of change inside, the end is in sight."

"Inside" means two things: inside the organization and inside the individual.

In either case, change begins inside an individual mind.

A Program for Personal Development

In the examples offered throughout this book, I have sought to convey that sentence-completion exercises can be powerful vehicles for self-understanding, self-discovery, and personal growth.

The program that follows has three basic purposes: to stimulate self-awareness, strengthen self-esteem, and ignite positive change.

The essence of the sentence-completion procedure, as we use it here, is to write an incomplete sentence, a sentence *stem*, and to keep adding different endings—between six and ten—with the sole requirement being that each ending be a grammatical completion of the sentence.

Work as rapidly as possible—no pauses to think, please. If you get stuck or your mind goes blank, invent. Don't worry if any particular ending is true, reasonable, or significant. Don't judge it. Any ending is fine. Just keep going.

The art of doing sentence completion well is to maintain a high level of mental focus combined with a complete lack of internal censorship. Doing sentence completion on a daily basis as described here is a kind of psychological discipline, a spiritual practice, even, that over time achieves insight, integration, and spontaneous behavior change.

People sometimes ask, "How do I integrate the things I am learning in sentence completion?" The answer is that the practice itself, done repetitively, brings about integration.

The speed of your progress depends in part on the level of focus and consciousness you bring to the work both while doing it and later when reviewing and reflecting on your endings.

When doing written rather than oral sentence-completion work, you can use a notebook, typewriter, or computer (although I am inclined to believe that handwriting is most effective).

Week 1

First thing in the morning, before proceeding to the day's business, sit down and write the following stem:

Personal growth to me means—

Then, as rapidly as possible, without pausing for reflection, write as many endings for that stem as you can in one or two minutes—never less than six, and ten is enough.

Don't worry about whether your endings make sense or seem sufficiently profound. Write anything but write something.

If you are a person with an inordinate need always to be in control, this may be difficult for you at first—because what is asked for here is spontaneity. But persevere. With practice it gets much easier.

Then, go on to the next stem:

If I brought 5 percent more self-esteem to my work—

Then:

If I brought 5 percent more self-esteem to my interactions with people—

Then:

If I want to grow in self-esteem I will need to—

When you have written six to ten endings for each of these stems, proceed with your day's business.

Do this exercise every day, Monday through Friday, for the first week, always before the start of the day's business.

Do not read what you wrote the day before. Naturally there will be repetitions. But also, new endings are inevitable.

Sometime each weekend, reread what you have written for the week. Reflect on it, and then write a minimum of six endings for this stem:

> **If any of what I wrote this week is true, it might be helpful if I—**

Continue this practice on the weekend throughout the entire program.

When doing the work, the ideal is to empty your mind of all expectations concerning what will happen or what is supposed to happen. Do not impose any demands on the situation. Do the exercise, go about the day's activities, and merely notice any differences in how you feel or how you act.

Remember: Your endings must be grammatical completions of the sentence, and if your mind blocks or goes absolutely empty, invent an ending, but do not allow yourself to stop with the thought that you cannot do the exercise.

An average session should not take longer than ten minutes. If it takes much longer, you are "thinking" (rehearsing, calculating) too much.

Week 2

If I operate 5 percent more consciously today—

If I am 5 percent more self-accepting today—

If I operate 5 percent more self-responsibly today—

If I operate 5 percent more self-assertively today—

If I operate 5 percent more purposefully today—

If I bring 5 percent more integrity to my activities today—

Week 3

If I bring 5 percent more awareness to my dealings with people today—

If I bring 5 percent more awareness to the quality of my communications—

If I bring 5 percent more awareness to my priorities today—

If I bring 5 percent more awareness to my most important tasks today—

Don't forget your weekend assignment.

Week 4

If I am 5 percent more self-accepting today—

If I am self-accepting even when I don't like what I am thinking or feeling—

If I am self-accepting even when I am miserable or confused—

If I can embrace the denied or disowned parts of myself—

Week 5

If I deal with others with respect and acceptance—

If I treat listening as a creative act—

When I notice how people are affected by the quality of my listening—

If I bring 5 percent more benevolence to my dealings with people—

Week 6

If I operate 5 percent more self-responsibly at work today—

If I operate 5 percent more self-responsibly in my dealings with people—

If I take responsibility for my choices and actions—

If I take responsibility for the attainment of my goals—

Week 7

If I operate 5 percent more self-assertively at work today—

If I operate 5 percent more self-assertively in my dealings with people—

If I combine self-assertiveness with benevolence—

If I treat my wants as important—

Week 8

If I bring 5 percent more purposefulness to my work today—

If I operate 5 percent more purposefully with people—

If I convert my wants and desires into conscious purposes—

When I don't operate purposefully at work—

When I don't operate purposefully in my relationships—

Don't forget your weekend assignment.

Week 9

If I bring 5 percent more integrity to my work—

If I bring 5 percent more integrity to my choices and actions—

If I want to admire my choices and actions I will need to—

When I don't act with integrity—

Week 10

If I operate 5 percent more consciously today—

If I am 5 percent more self-accepting today—

If I operate 5 percent more self-responsibly today—

If I operate 5 percent more self-assertively today—

If I operate 5 percent more purposefully today—

If I bring 5 percent more integrity to my activities today—

Week 11

If the child in me could speak, that child would say—

If the teenager I once was still exists inside of me—

If my teenaged self could speak, that youth would say—

At the thought of reaching back to help my child-self—

At the thought of reaching back to help my teenaged self—

Don't forget your weekend assignment.

Week 12

If I could make friends with my younger selves—

If my child-self felt accepted by me—

If my teen-aged self felt accepted by me—

If my younger selves felt I had compassion for their struggles—

Week 13

If I were to embrace all the younger parts of me—

If my younger selves are rejected by me—

One of the ways my child-self can get back at me for rejection is—

One of the ways my teen-aged self can get back at me for rejection is—

If I want to feel whole and undivided—

Week 14

If I accept responsibility for my choices and actions—

If I accept responsibility for how I deal with people—

If I accept responsibility for the words coming out of my mouth—

If I were willing to be fully accountable for my promises and my actions—

Week 15

When I operate more consciously I notice that I—

When I operate more self-acceptingly I notice that I—

When I operate more self-responsibly I notice that I—

When I operate more self-assertively I notice that I—

When I operate more purposefully I notice that I—

When I operate with more integrity I notice that I—

Week 16

I am motivated to give my best when—

If I want to inspire others to give their best—

If I want to be perceived as fair and just—

If I want to be perceived as trustworthy—

If I want to be perceived as benevolent—

Week 17

I work best with others when I—

If I want other people to feel visible to me—

If I want other people to enjoy working with me—

If I take full responsibility for the quality of my communications—

Week 18

If I don't blame, alibi, or make myself confused—

If I focus on what needs to be done rather than on my self-doubts—

If I refuse to engage in personality clashes—

If I take full responsibility for how I prioritize—

If I am willing to see what I see and know what I know—

Week 19

If I reread this book in a state of full consciousness—

If I focus on how I can translate the ideas in this book into action—

If I approach work as a vehicle for personal growth and development—

If I approach every day as an opportunity to grow in self-esteem—

Week 20

If I operate 5 percent more consciously today—

If I am 5 percent more self-accepting today—

If I operate 5 percent more self-responsibly today—

If I operate 5 percent more self-assertively today—

If I operate 5 percent more purposefully today—

If I bring 5 percent more integrity to my activities today—

Week 21

If I want to use the ideas in this book as guides for personal development—

If I want to translate what I am learning into action—

If I make self-development my conscious purpose—

If I am willing to see what I see and know what I know—

I am becoming aware—

Moving On

Suggestion: When you have completed all twenty-one weeks of this program, take a week off and then do the program again, from the beginning, as if you had never done it before. You may be surprised in the changes in many of your responses, which will give you some indication of the progress you are making . . . as well as obstacles to growth you may need to work at overcoming.

Working in Groups

In some organizations, people like to meet in small groups late on Friday afternoon to share their endings for the week, explore implications, review progress, and brainstorm on ways to translate new learnings into new behaviors. Sometimes an entire department breaks up into groups of not more than four people for this purpose.

In such groups there is no leader—everyone is viewed as and treated as an equal on the path of self-development. The focus is always on the action implications of new realizations.

A Final Word

For further self-development work I recommend the personal growth programs in my books *The Six Pillars of Self-Esteem*, *Taking Responsibility*, and *The Art of Living Consciously*.

Notes

Chapter One

1. *Fortune*, December 17, 1990.
2. New York: Little, Brown, 1973, p. 62.
3. New York: Simon & Schuster, 1996, pp. 198–221.
4. Quoted in *The Economist*, December 1, 1990.
5. Daniel Goleman, *Emotional Intelligence*. New York: Bantam Books, 1997.

Chapter Two

1. For misconceptions and misrepresentations concerning self-esteem, see my discussion in Chapter 6 of *The Art of Living Consciously*. New York: Simon & Schuster, 1997.
2. For a discussion of these correlations, see Nathaniel Branden, *The Six Pillars of Self-Esteem*, pp. 44–48. New York: Bantam Books, 1994.

Chapter Three

1. Reprinted in *Leaders on Leadership*, edited by Warren Bennis. Cambridge, Mass.: Harvard Business Review Press, 1992, pp. 16–17.
2. Quoted in James O'Toole, *Leading Change*. San Francisco: Jossey-Bass, 1995, p. 148.

3. See Warren Bennis and Burt Nanus, *Leaders*, revised edition. New York: HarperBusiness, 1997.
4. Quoted in *Leading Change*, by James O'Toole. San Francisco: Jossey-Bass, 1995, p. 59.

Chapter Four

1. A more detailed discussion of how one creates an organizational culture of high accountability is offered in my *Taking Responsibility*, New York: Simon & Schuster, 1996.
2. Reported in the *Wall Street Journal*, May 2, 1988.

About the Author

With a Ph.D. in psychology and a background in philosophy, Nathaniel Branden is a practicing psychotherapist in Los Angeles, and, in addition, does corporate consulting all over the world, conducting seminars, workshops, and conferences on the application of self-esteem principles and technology to the challenges of modern business. He is the author of many books, including *The Six Pillars of Self-Esteem*, *Taking Responsibility*, and *The Art of Living Consciously*. His work has been translated into fourteen languages and there are more than three million copies of his books in print.

In addition to his in-person practice, he consults via the telephone worldwide. He can be reached through his Los Angeles office at:

P.O. Box 2609
Beverly Hills, CA 90213
Telephone: (310) 274-6361
Fax: (310) 271-6808
E-Mail: NathanielBranden@compuserve.com
Web site: http://www.nathanielbranden.net

Index